What a gem of a book this is for writers! Linda is such an incredible resource, and I love her passion for helping us to use our God-given voices in so many ways to reach and serve others I'm partial to podcasting and as an avid fan of Linda's own show, I know she sets the bar high as a host and in serving her audience. What a blessing that we can now all learn her tips and tricks and lessons of excellence.

—***Kim Stewart***
Marketing Strategist,
Host of Book Marketing Mania

If you're a faith-based writer considering the venture into podcasting, Linda Goldfarb's *Creating Dynamic Podcasts & Audiobooks* is an essential roadmap. With years of experience behind her innovative and award-winning podcasts, Linda shares her expert knowledge in a way that's insightful and practical.

This book doesn't just tell you why podcasting is valuable, it shows you how. It's filled with actionable advice that gave me the confidence to prepare for my own podcast endeavors.

Whether you aim to guest on podcasts or create your own, you'll find *Creating Dynamic Podcasts & Audiobooks* an invaluable asset in your journey. The book is a confidence-builder and a strategy adviser rolled into one. I highly recommend this resource for anyone wanting to harness the power of podcasting to amplify their message.

—Christine Hoy
Speaker, Author, Coach

If you're looking for someone to walk you through the process of how to podcast or narrate books with confidence and success, THIS IS IT! Whether you're just starting out or wanting to deepen your understanding to improve your strategy and skills, Linda Goldfarb's *Creating Dynamic Podcasts & Audiobooks* offers a clear, strategic path to success for you to follow. This step-by-step guide isn't only for faith-based communicators or writers, but for anyone wanting to expand their reach through the world of podcasting and book narration.

This go-to guide, written by an award-winning seasoned expert, is a must-have for anyone who aspires to excel in podcasting and the art of book narration. Unlock your potential and expand your reach with this invaluable resource.

—Dr. Sharon O'Hara
Speaker, Blogger, and Host of *Be the 25* Podcast

Linda's deep commitment to serving the Christian writing community radiates throughout *Creating Dynamic Podcasts & Audiobooks* as she generously imparts years of knowledge and experience to her readers. This book is a treasure trove of expert guidance, offering a comprehensive masterclass on audio content creation for writers. Whether you are a beginner or an experienced professional in podcasting, audiobooks, or public speaking, there are valuable insights tailored to your skill level that you can immediately apply. Linda skillfully navigates the technical aspects, practical tips, and more, crafting a valuable reference that you can turn to time and again. Through her authentic and relatable writing style, you will be inspired, empowered, and emboldened to amplify your *Creating Dynamic Podcasts & Audiobooks* for the greater glory of God.

—Jenny Leavitt
Award-winning Author,
Board-Certified Mental Health Coach

I didn't fully understand insecurity until I became a writer. It wasn't until I ventured into the world of audiobooks that I experienced the hide-under-the-desk panic. Decisions from the right voice to marketing loomed large. Thankfully, Linda's expertise calmed my verklempt heart. *Creating Dynamic Podcasts & Audiobooks* should sit on every writer's reference bookshelf.

—Robin Luftig
Author of *God's Best During Your Worst*

I wish every author would read *Creating Dynamic Podcasts & Audiobooks* and follow Linda's guidelines to a T. Having produced seventeen audiobooks over the past three years, I've partnered with both flexible and rigid authors. The most challenging working relationships result from partnering with an author who assumes a narrator's clairvoyance. I need to know everything my authors can tell me about their story world, characters, and the book's takeaway prior to, not during, production. Implementing Linda's practical and invaluable audiobook worksheets would create beautiful working relationships between authors and narrators.

—Christy Lou
Professional Audiobook Narrator,
Author of *Freeing Colt* as Christy Lindsay

Linda Goldfarb's book is like having the best of the best providing you step-by-step instructions and insider tips. What a gift for podcasters and audiobook authors/narrators.

—Cheri Cowell
Founder/CEO EABooks Publishing

If I had *Create Dynamic Podcasts & Audiobooks* by Linda Goldfarb before launching StoryJumpers (and several other podcasts on The Bridge Podcast Network), I would have saved a lot of time, frustration, and expense. I would be a lot further ahead, too! Fortunately, with her well-organized book, I can target shortcomings and improve our entire library of content to reach the ideal listener and achieve the results we desire."

—Andrew Jackson
StoryJumpers Host

THE WRITER'S BOOKSHELF

Creating Dynamic Podcasts & Audiobooks

LINDA GOLDFARB

Bold Vision Books
PO Box 2011
Friendswood, Texas 77549

ISBN: 9781962705226

Published by Bold Vision Books, PO Box 2011, Friendswood, Texas 77549
www.boldvisionbooks.com

Edited by Larry J. Leech II
Cover Design by Amber Wiegand-Buckley, Barefaced Media and Lisa Burns

Interior design by WendyEL Creative

Published in the United States of America.

This book is a labor of love for fellow creatives who desire to have their voices heard beyond the pages of their writings. May Father use each word to make a difference in the reader's life for His glory.

CONTENTS

Foreword 11
Introduction 17

PODCASTING AND THE FAITH-BASED WRITER 23

(1) What is Podcasting? 25
(2) Identify Your Listening Audience 31
(3) Listen to Podcasts 39
(4) Create Top Three Interview Topics 41
(5) Create Promise-based Interview Questions 45
(6) Create Professional Interview Query Sheet 53
(7) Identify Your Podcasting Personality 59
(8) The Mobilizer-Leader 63
(9) The Socializer-Talker 67
(10) The Stabilizer-Peacekeeper 71
(11) The Organizer-Thinker 75
(12) Choose Your Podcast Mission 79
(13) Mission Choices 85
(14) Choose Your Podcast Format 89
(15) Choose Your Podcast Name 95
(16) Choose Your Podcast Brand 105

(17) Create Your Podcast Content 111
(18) Create Your Podcast Guest Interview Sheet . 123
(19) Choose Your Podcast Hosting Service 127
(20) Choose Podcast Editing and Recording Equipment 131
(21) Always Be Teachable 135
(22) Enlist a Coach 149

AUDIOBOOKS AND THE FAITH-BASED WRITER 155

(23) What Are Audiobooks? 157
(24) Consider Your Audience Demographics 161
(25) Be Discoverable 165
(26) Choose the Best Voice 167
(27) The Matter of Money 179
(28) Market Your Audiobook Effectively 185
(29) Make Your Book Audio Ready 189

Endnotes 203
Acknowledgements 205
Meet Linda 209

Foreword

Through Spark Media, I've had the honor of helping hundreds of award-winning Christian podcasters and communicators develop their God given message, grow their influence, and step into their calling as a Christian communicator. Spark Media is a leading force in the podcast industry, dedicated to fostering creativity, innovation, and excellence in Christian podcasting.

I met Linda Goldfarb the year I launched the award-winning The Struggle is Real But so is God Bible Study and the By His Grace podcast, just months before God called me to launch Spark Media. It was at the Blue Ridge Mountains Christian Writers Conference where Linda, with a masterful command of oratory, was conducting a speaking masterclass. Her voice, rich and captivating, effortlessly commanded attention, weaving the intricate tapestry of bold and confident communication with threads of humor and wit. Identifying the various traits of communicators.

Her ability to make the complex art of public speaking engaging and entertaining was nothing short of inspirational. The following year she attended the inaugural Spark conference for Christian podcasters and joined the Spark Media Collective training community. The rest is history!

Friends, words have power. It is no coincidence that when God created the world, He spoke it into existence. "In the beginning, God created the heavens and the earth. The earth was without form and void, and darkness was over the face of the deep. And the Spirit of God was hovering over the face of the waters. And God said, "Let there be light," and there was light" (Genesis 1:1-3). Scripture also teaches us in Proverbs 18:21 there is power in our tongues to speak life or death.

The power of our voice is truly remarkable. It's not just a tool for communication; it's a profound instrument of influence and hope. When we speak, the words we share impart wisdom, and knowledge to inspire others, and advocate for our beliefs. Our words are powerful and can be life-giving to others. We can offer comfort, joy, and peace to a world that desperately needs it. We have the incredible opportunity to share the gospel through podcasting and audio books, thus fulfilling the great commission.

In *Creating Dynamic Podcasts & Audiobooks*, Linda gives you the tools you need to use your voice to be a force for good to launch a podcast, become a podcast guest, or create an audiobook with excellence.

In today's world, the impact of our voice is amplified like never before through podcasting and the spoken word to make a global impact. We have the power to reach a global audience, to be part of meaningful conversations, and to contribute to making the world a better place. Our voice carries our personal stories and experiences, making each of us uniquely influential. It's a reflection of our thoughts, beliefs, and values. We educate, inspire, and entertain others when we share our stories. On these pages you will find best practices to share your story to give God glory with Linda's expertise as your guide.

This book serves as a comprehensive guide for faith-based writers venturing into the realm of podcasting and audiobook creation. In the first part, Linda demystifies podcasting, beginning with a fundamental explanation of the medium and progressing through a series of best practices tailored for those aiming to guest on podcasts. She advocates understanding one's audience, advises on listening to existing podcasts, and emphasizes the need for crafting engaging interview topics and questions, along with preparing a professional interview query sheet.

The hosting section delves into personal podcasting styles, identifying various personality types such as the Mobilizer-Leader, Socializer-Talker,

Stabilizer-Peacekeeper, and Organizer-Thinker, and how these traits influence podcasting dynamics. Linda provides a step-by-step strategy for defining the podcast's mission, format, name, and brand, as well as creating content, guest interview intake sheets, and selecting the right hosting service and technical equipment. She also emphasizes the importance of continuous learning, seeking mentorship, and maintaining a teachable spirit rounds out the hosting advice.

The second part transitions into the creation and promotion of audiobooks, addressing the significance of audiobooks in today's market and outlining key practices for success. Linda stresses the importance of knowing the audience demographics, ensuring discoverability, selecting the appropriate voice, understanding financial considerations, and strategizing the marketing of audiobooks. Additionally, she guides writers on how to make their books suitable for audio adaptation.

The book concludes with resources to support faith-based writers on their journey into podcasting and audiobooks, offering tools and guidance for effective communication in the digital age.

This book emerges as an invaluable resource for faith-based writers who are navigating, or want to navigate, the burgeoning fields of podcasting and audiobooks. It blends pragmatic advice with a deep understanding of the spiritual and communicative goals that such writers strive for, offering a unique blend of technical guidance, marketing wisdom, and spiritual insight. It's more than just a how-to manual; it's a navigator for the digital storytelling space, tailored specifically for those who intertwine their craft with their faith.

Let's remember that with great power comes great responsibility. At this moment on the Kingdom calendar, it's crucial to use our voice to express the hope that lies within us. Using our voice thoughtfully can foster understanding and empathy, bridging gaps between diverse perspectives, all the while pointing people to Jesus. Let's cherish this opportunity to use our voice wisely, recognizing its power to influence, and inspire.

Your voice matters, and you can make a difference in this world! I can't wait to see what you create!

Much Love and By His Grace,
Misty Phillip
Founder and CEO of Spark Media and
Spark Media Ventures

Introduction

Are you ready for this? I trust that Father God has you reading *Creating Dynamic Podcasts & Audiobooks* because your writing journey has brought you to a crossroads. Which direction is your next best step? Guesting on or hosting a podcast? Turning your manuscript into an audiobook? Both?

In the pages that follow, you receive an overflow of possibilities. I'm a firm believer that the Holy Spirit has prepared you for this point in your career as a faith-based writer. He has guided you. Inspired you. Encouraged you and equipped you—for this season. All you need to do is gain knowledge, learn a skill or two, and apply what you learn in accordance with Father's way, will, and timing.

If you agree that your next best step could include podcasting and / or audiobooks, I'm excited for you. You never know what Father has in store but be assured that where you are right now is not a surprise to Him.

I doubt my parents ever imagined how Father would use the loud voice of their energetic middle child to impact His kingdom. I find it delightful when Father shows signs of who He's designed us to be from a young age. Perhaps you started writing in grade school and your ability to write seemed as natural as your ability to walk. For me, it was my inherent ability to talk in front of people that sprung forth early on.

The phrases I heard most often from my parents or people of authority were "Linda, you need to calm down just a little bit." "Shh, it's not your turn to talk." Yep. Natural talker here.

Similar words graced the comment sections in my report cards each year until one of my fifth-grade teachers redirected the chain of observations. "One day, Linda's voice will make an impact on others greater than we can imagine now." Wow. I believe the Holy Spirit was at work in my teacher to encourage me when I needed reassurance of who I was designed to be. The proof is evident in all I do today.

My voice is a resource of far-reaching communication. For ten years, I hosted *Not Just Talkin' the Talk*—a talk radio program which debuted on KSLR, a Salem affiliate, in San Antonio, Texas. The show grew to a regional syndication and then to world-wide distribution through Blog Talk Radio. I currently speak and perform in the U.S. and internationally. I'm blessed to have a few audiobook narration projects under my belt, as they make great use of the various dialects and vocal prowess I've mastered over the years.

And I'm honored to emcee the Blue Ridge Mountains Christian Writers Conference, the highest-attended Christian writers conference in the United States averaging more than 600 onsite attendees annually. Lastly, as the podcasting host of *Your Best Writing Life* and *Staying Real About Faith & Family*, it's a joy to speak into the lives of faith-based writers and families to encourage their professional and personal best.

LITERACY IS AN AUDIBLE COMMODITY.

My passion for equipping writers and living the writer's life personally is one of the main reasons for penning *Creating Dynamic Podcasts & Audiobooks*. While you map out your future podcasting and audiobook journey, be encouraged, your words have the potential to reach far beyond the pen and into the ears of your readers enhancing their knowledge with your expertise. Literacy is an audible commodity you can take advantage of.

As faith-based writers, we are called to speak into the lives of Christ followers and seekers, those who currently know him and those who are yet to know the eternal blessing of salvation.

Creating Dynamic Podcasts & Audiobooks is designed to speak hope into the lives of friends, family, and at times, strangers. Yet, the readers of our books, blog posts, and articles reflect a mere portion of who we can inspire, equip, and encourage with our voice. So, how do we reach the remnant? Through podcasts and audiobooks.

Whether we are confident in our literal voices or timid about projecting vocally, podcasts and audiobooks are here to stay. These are effective tools to increase our reach. The practices in this book will guide you to your next best step to utilize the message you are equipped to share with a larger audience.

You will walk away knowing the best practices of podcasting from guesting to hosting and concept to production. And the best practices of audiobook narration from how your book fits, choosing the best narrator, and how to market the completed project to your current readers.

While you read through the best practices of podcasting and audiobooks, I suggest you fill in as many of the blanks as you can the first go round, then listen for Father's leading. He will prompt you to move forward at just the right time.

Consider *Creating Dynamic Podcasts & Audiobooks* a resource to revisit often as Father grows you and increases your territory.

As a board-certified Christian life coach, it's exciting for me to journey with you as you grow your platform into the fabulous world of hearable resources. Podcasts and audiobooks can powerfully change the lives of your current readers while extending your reach and message into the world of fellow followers of Christ.

Reach out and let me know how Father moves you forward to increase the reach of your writer's voice. I'm just an email away.

Hugs in Him,

Linda

PODCASTING

AND THE

FAITH-BASED WRITER

"I had much to write to you, but I would rather not write with pen and ink."

(3 John 1:13)

(((1)))

WHAT IS PODCASTING?

Before you step behind the mic as a podcast guest or invest your finances into this industry as a host, take a moment to shorten your learning curve and gain an insider's insight into the world of podcasting.

WHAT IS PODCASTING?

Podcasting is the new radio of the twenty-first century.

Making its debut in the 1920s, radio broadcasting was heard daily in homes and on the road while individuals went to and from work. Today we have numerous audio options beyond radio vying for the attention of listeners. Podcasts are on the increase and impacting families at home and during transit.

As a rule, podcasts are audio files accessed online via apps or through a web browser. Podcasting hosts post audio episodes ranging from a couple of minutes to more than an hour in length. Some podcasts provide video access to their episodes, but for the most part, audio alone is an acceptable source for listeners.

As a listener, you are encouraged to subscribe to a podcast by clicking yes, subscribe, or follow on the platform of your choosing via your mobile device or computer. Subscribing ensures that every episode is downloaded into your app for your listening convenience.

According to the Pew Research Center, "Americans listen to podcasts to learn, for entertainment, and to fill time while doing other things."[1]

Listeners value current events, editorials, education, inspiration, and opinion as listen worthy. Source: Survey of U.S. adults conducted Dec. 5-11. 2022 "Podcasts as a Source of News and Information"

	MAIN PURPOSE	SECONDARY PURPOSE
Entertainment	60%	27%
Education	55%	33%
Fill time	52%	29%
Opinion Editorial	30%	41%
Current Events	29%	34%
Inspiration	27%	32%

While radio holds a place in the audio space, according to survey data from Edison Research, online audio such as podcasts are on the rise. "As of early 2023,

75 percent of Americans ages twelve and older have listened to online audio in the past month, while 70 percent have listened in the past week." [2]

Those who listen to podcasts do so for variety of reasons. Most podcast listeners between 18 to 29 years old tune in for entertainment and to fill time while doing something else. Podcast listeners over the age of 65 listen primarily to learn.[3]

DOES PODCASTING RESONATE WITH CHRISTIAN LISTENERS?

If you wonder about your ability to influence Christian listeners, be encouraged. According to a 2023 article from one of the top podcasting platforms, blubrry.com, "Religious podcasts listenership has grown at an astronomical rate."[4] In fact, "Over the past decade, Religious podcast listeners (as measured by downloads) has increased by 85 percent. On average. Per year. 85 percent. That's a phenomenal growth rate. Interesting side note: most of that enormous growth rate happened in 2015, when we saw a jump from roughly 110M downloads in Q1 2014 to nearly 680M estimated downloads in Q4 2015. If we remove that anomalous year, the growth rate *still* averages nearly 30 percent per year, which is nearly *triple* the average growth rate of all podcast estimated downloads."

A few examples of podcast listeners and what they look for:

> "I listen to podcasts daily for three reasons, to learn new insights, for entertainment/humor during times I need a pick-me-up, and to support writer and speaker friends."—Teresa Moyer

> "I listen to podcasts several times a week while I'm walking, driving, or doing chores. I like to learn something new, to be inspired and encouraged, and I appreciate it when they're also entertaining."—Christine Hoy

> "I listen to podcasts on a weekly basis to gain knowledge, spark inspiration, prompt personal growth, and hear other's perspectives."—Lisa Robbins

> "I educationally listen to podcasts/watch YT videos for two main reasons. 1. Gain information on topics I am unfamiliar with but interested in. 2. Gain exposure to more anecdotes and personal stories related to particular topics."—Steve Stuve

Podcasting is here to stay and it's a viable outlet to reach faith-based listeners, your readers. The time is now to begin your podcasting path of influence. Follow the contents of this book and take your first step.

Before hosting a podcast get your feet wet by guesting on one. The following five best practices help to kick start your podcasting career as a successful guest. Having these practices in place prior to guesting on or hosting a podcast will make you a better host and a much sought-after guest.

BEST PRACTICES

TO

GUEST ON A PODCAST

(((2)))

BEST GUESTING PRACTICE 1

Identify Your Listening Audience

Many new authors, eager to get their information into the media, make a common mistake. They send interview queries to podcasts that don't fit their personality or the focus of their mission. Chapters two and three will equip you with information to protect you from making this common mistake. Identifying our audience keeps us focused and moving forward.

Before we can identify our potential audiences, we need to clarify our core message or theme. As you adventure into podcasting think of multiple ideas your topic can cover to reach wider audiences in addition to the obvious ones.

As a podcast guest, you are more than one book, one article, one poem, or one writing credit of any kind. You are now the writer who thinks with a series in mind. And the most important aspect of adopting a series mindset is creating conversational topics that give the listener's needs top priority.

I'm the author of the *LINKED® Quick Guide to Personalities* series. As of this writing there are four books in the series: *LINKED® The Quick Guide to Personalities, LINKED® for Educators, LINKED® for Parents,* and *LINKED® for Couples.*

Promoting the original *LINKED® Quick Guide* opened numerous opportunities for me to speak and teach on the subject of personalities. This guide also won the 2019 Non-fiction Book of the Year via the Golden Scrolls Awards held in Nashville, TN, giving my coauthor Linda Gilden and me credibility in our field of expertise.

Before the additional books were written, I guested on several podcasts, radio programs, and television shows sharing a message of hope for better communication in relationships. The media programs I interviewed with had different audiences, and though I had one book, I formatted my content to meet the needs of each show based on the premise of better communication.

To answer what's in it for your listeners, identify four factors:

- Your core message
- Who are your listeners
- What your listeners need
- How you can meet your listener's needs

WHAT IS YOUR CORE MESSAGE?

As an author who now thinks beyond your book, take a moment to identify the core message of your writing. Your core message could be helping people with better communication, as in my *LINKED®* books, or finding hope when life gets complicated, as in *Soul Care When You're Weary* by Edie Melson, or establishing church unity as in *Crazy Love: Overwhelmed by a Relentless God* by Francis Chan or practical help for single moms as in *The 10 Best Decisions a Single Mom Can Make* by Pam Farrel and PeggySue Wells.

Write your core message in ten words or less in the space below. Keep in mind that simple is always better.

MY CORE MESSAGE:

____

____

____

____

____

WHICH AUDIENCES WILL BENEFIT FROM YOUR CORE MESSAGE?

As the author, search for the specific categories, such as parenting, leadership, couples, wellness or your topic to find podcasts that interview guests on these subjects. Using the books previously mentioned, here are a few podcast audiences the authors might consider guesting on.

LINKED® - Families, leaders, and parents.

Soul Care When You're Weary - Caregivers, educators, and pastors

Crazy Love - Church congregations, families, and Christians

The 10 Best Decisions a Single Mom Can Make - Moms, parents, and churches

Based on the examples listed, what three audiences would your topics be well suited for?

MY THREE AUDIENCES ARE:

Audience 1:

___

Audience 2:

___

Audience 3:

___

WHAT DO THESE AUDIENCES NEED?

Here are a few needs each audience has from the previous examples:

- Families need to adopt better communication skills for relationships to thrive.
- Leaders need to learn better communication skills to increase productivity.
- Church congregations need a spiritual revival.
- Christians need relational encouragement.
- Caregivers need encouragement to take care of themselves.
- Pastors need creative ways to relax.
- Parents need to know how to thrive as a single parent family.
- Church communities need to know how to assist single parents in their congregation better.

BASED ON THE EXAMPLES, WHAT NEEDS DO YOUR THREE AUDIENCES HAVE THAT YOU CAN SERVE?

Audience 1:

___

___

___

Audience 2:

___

___

___

Audience 3:

HOW DOES YOUR CONTENT MEET YOUR AUDIENCE'S NEEDS?

Here are ways the core message of the beforementioned books can meet the needs of their audiences.

LINKED® offers families an assessment to identify who's living under their roof and three strategies to best connect with each personality.

LINKED® offers leaders a personality assessment that's easy to understand with three strategies to help differing personalities be more effective in their positions.

Soul Care When You're Weary offers caregivers creative ways to unload their daily burdens to better care for themselves.

Soul Care offers pastors and their teams creative ways to step away and recoup without leaving town.

Crazy Love: Overwhelmed by a Relentless God offers congregations a video series for extended training.

Crazy Love offers Christians five ways to extend love to one another.

The 10 Best Decisions a Single Mom Can Make offers parents, biblical truths with practical applications to make everyday life less stressful.

10-Best offers church communities seven ways to come alongside single parents with practical and relational applications.

LIST HOW YOUR CONTENT CAN SATISFY THE NEEDS OF YOUR THREE AUDIENCES:

Audience 1:

____

____

____

Audience 2:

____

____

____

Audience 3:

____

____

____

The next best practice as a podcast guest is to listen to a variety of podcasts that cater to your audiences to determine if their listeners need your expertise.

BEST GUESTING PRACTICE 2

Listen to Podcasts

Though time consuming, listening to podcasts prepares you to be an outstanding guest in ways you can only learn from studying fellow podcasters and documenting the techniques and styles that might fit you and your mission.

Begin by searching the internet for podcasts that cater to your audience. At first glance we may think easy peasy, search and find. Unless you're not exactly sure who your audience is. It's imperative that you understand and implement the principles found in Identify Your Listening Audience first, then come back to this section.

PODCASTING PLATFORMS

Podcasting platforms are the apps where podcasts are found. In this growing industry, new hosting platforms continue to pop up everywhere. A few platforms that look like they will be around for the extended future of podcasting include:

Apple Podcast
Spotify
RSS Feed
Amazon Music

When you find the platform that fits you, as in Apple Podcast for MacBook, iPhone, and iPad users, as Apple Podcast is built into these systems, search for interview-formatted programs that feed into the lives of your audiences. For Android users, Google Podcasts and Podcast Addict are two of the top apps. Listen to several programs to discover the interview style of the host.

A bonus best practice. Leave a review for the shows you may want to guest on. Mention something about the episode you heard and be authentic and considerate in what you say. Always give honest reviews, it's what you expect and desire from others for your future podcast. And subscribe to the podcast. By subscribing, you can keep track of episodes that precede yours. This knowledge will help you with the topics you pitch.

Now let's flesh out the topics to pitch.

(((4)))

BEST GUESTING PRACTICE 3

Create Top Three Interview Topics

Effective interview topics are honed to attract specific audiences. For practical purposes, concentrate on one audience from your list when you fill in the requested information. Choose the one that you are most passionate about. Passion carries a lot of interview weight—this is the topic you can speak about in your sleep. When you have this topic fleshed out, do the same with any future topic.

For simplicity of example, I'll use families for my passion topic based on the book *LINKED*®. Recall "*LINKED*® offers families an assessment to identify who's living under their roof and three strategies to best connect with each personality." Based on this topic I create a title. Note that the podcast host may choose a title they prefer, but if you offer them a great title that speaks to the need of their listeners you make the host's job easier.

The topic title reveals the promised content offered to podcast hosts and their listeners. I use Headline Analyzer (HA) to find the title that resonates intellectually with the highest percentage of my listeners. A link to the Headline Analyzer that I use is found in Resources.

THE TOPIC TITLE REVEALS THE PROMISED CONTENT OFFERED.

Three topic/titles for a family interview. I look for 50 percent connection rate or higher.

Three Ways to Help Families Talk Things Out–HA 50 percent

Three Ways to Help Families Get Along–HA 57.14 percent

Three Strategies to Help Families to be Less Combative–HA 88.89 percent

All these topics rank well. I would include these topics in my query and the host will make the selection. I include three to five talking points per topic for the host to choose from. Based on your one audience and how your content can satisfy their need, write out three topic titles and search them on Headline Analysis. Add, subtract, and replace words in Headline to fine-tune your promise for highest engagement. Place the Headline Analysis connection percentage after each title.

List your three titles here:

Topic title 1: ____________________

Topic title 2: ____________________

Topic title 3: ____________________

If you come up with more than three, that's okay too. The next step is to create promise-based questions.

(((5)))

BEST GUESTING PRACTICE 4

Create Promise-based Interview Questions

As an interviewer, my top priority is to satisfy the needs of my audience. The first question I ask myself: "What do I say at the top of the interview to keep listeners tuned in?" I offer a question or two that we will answer during the episode, and then, of course, I make sure they get answered.

The second priority is to hold the attention of my listeners. Podcast hosts hold the attention of our listeners by fulfilling the promise we said we would provide in the episode title. Crafting promise-based interview questions do just that. Most authors have good questions, but often the questions deal with the authors and their story rather than being directed to the need of the audience. I like to use "ear tinglers"—thought provokers. Most interviews last between twenty-five to forty-five minutes.

What you give the interviewer to say will open your opportunity to share the essence of your message, sell your book, gain email subscribers, and grow your social media followers. Your questions need to promise answers to the needs of the listeners.

Go back to the Identify Your Listening Audience chapter and write in your answers below:

First Interview topic________________________

____

____

Interview audience for first topic____________

____

____

Need of your listeners for first topic________

____

____

Keep your answers in mind when you read an example of interview questions for my *LINKED® Quick Guide to Personalities* book.

Interview Topic: Three Areas Personality Knowledge Provides Better Communication in Busy Families (HA 80 percent)

Interview talking points/questions I give the host:

1. Linda, you say the LINKED® Personality assessment helps busy families (my audience) experience better communication (their need). Give us an overview of the four personalities. I see you have Mobilizers, Socializers, Stabilizers, and Organizers.

In answer to this question asked by the host, I give a concise summary.

2. How has the LINKED® personality knowledge helped you personally?
3. What are the three ways parents will experience better communication using personality knowledge?

Bonus: What final thoughts would you like to leave with our listeners?

Using my interview questions as a template, write three of your own plus a bonus question. Use the beginning prompts provided if needed.

Name of your book:______________________________
Topic of the interview:___________________________
Interview questions you will give the host:

1. (insert your name), you say (insert book title) can help our listeners (insert the need of listener it will help). Where do we begin?
2. How can…or what steps…

3. How has…

Bonus: What final thoughts would you like to leave with our listeners? (Have one or two answers prepared).

Now repeat this process for your additional topics.

2–Name of your book:____________________________

Topic of the interview:__________________________

Interview questions you will give the host:

1. (insert your name), you say (insert book title) can help our listeners (insert the need of listener it will help). Where do we begin?
2. How can…or what steps…
3. How has…

Bonus: What final thoughts would you like to leave with our listeners?

3–Name of your book:____________________________

Topic of the interview:__________________________

Interview questions you will give the host:

1. (insert your name), you say (insert book title) can help our listeners (insert the need of listener it will help). Where do we begin?
2. How can…or what steps…
3. How has…

Bonus: What final thoughts would you like to leave with our listeners?

Now you have three topics with quality questions to help the podcast hosts conduct a valuable interview that engages and benefits listeners.

Provide your host with an updated headshot, current fifty-word bio, book cover jpeg, and social media links. Also, include a link to your media page.

CREATE YOUR MEDIA PAGE

Great interviewees make the host's job easy. One way to do this is to provide a designated web address for media (podcast, radio, bloggers, and television hosts) to locate your resources. This page should be integrated into your main website. Most often the Media page is an extension like what I have on my website LindaGoldfarb.com/media.

A Media page for the purpose of interviews should include the following:

- Two or three headshots in high resolution color, low resolution color, and black and white. Check out LindaGoldfarb.com/media for my personal examples.
- Contact Link to book the interview.
- Information about your book(s). This can be on an additional one sheet or in the body of the webpage.
- Sample interview topics with questions.

- Awards associated with the book, your topic, and or your personal and professional accomplishments.

Your media page doesn't have to be extravagant to be effective. The items listed above provide a good start for any interested media person. The host will ask for additional information, if they need any, when you are booked for the interview.

If you have not created a main website, Thomas Umstattd Jr., offers a free course on how to make your author website. Here's the link address training.authormedia.com/p/amazing-author-websites

CREATE YOUR AUDIENCE LEAD MAGNET/GIVEAWAY

What ancillary giveaway or Lead Magnet can you easily provide for the listeners after they've heard your interview? Lead Magnets offer useful tools or valuable information in exchange for the listeners email address. With their email contact, you can connect with the listener directly with future content in their area of interest.

Another best practice as a podcast guest, is to always give the listeners high-value information. Don't hoard your knowledge. Don't fear giving away the farm. Giving high-value information during your interview draws listeners to connect with you for more great content.

You *must* have an email marketing provider for your website, such as MailerLite, Constant Contact, Mailchimp, ConvertKit, or AWeber. Any digital idea that is easily downloadable makes for an excellent giveaway.

- A Hot Topic Sheet. Your Top (select a number) Ways to… in a PDF format One Sheet
- A Digital Quick Guide. Up to fifteen pages in a PDF format
- A Digital Booklet. Up to fifty pages in a PDF format
- An Audio Download. An audio containing information pertinent to your topic in a MP3 format
- A Video Download. Teach a how-to or provide some form of entertainment in a MP4 format

(((6)))

BEST GUESTING PRACTICE 5

Create Professional Interview Query Sheet

With everything in place to begin your interview, it's time to reach out to podcast hosts who have an audience you can serve.

Begin with a query email. This is a pitch to the host as to why you are a good fit for their program. When creating your podcast query, be concise in your offering and include:

- Who you are – fifty words or less
- What you do – fifty words or less
- Why you are a good guest for this specific show – list three of your topics

- What you are an expert on – bullet points
- Your contact information
- Your professional headshot – be sure your personality shines in your photo
- Your professional website link

IF THE PODCAST HAS SPECIFIC QUERY GUIDELINES, THESE TRUMP ANYTHING ELSE. SEND WHAT IS REQUESTED IN THE FORMAT SPECIFIED.

If the podcast has specific query guidelines, these trump everything else. Send what is requested in the format requested.

As a host, I prefer the headshot and book cover jpegs as attachments. This format allows me to save them separately into a file for ease of posting on my website and in my podcasting provider.

Be sure to email the correct person. Usually, you find the booking contact information on the podcast website or in the description of the podcast on the podcasting platform.

In addition to the query or pitch, develop a one-sheet that includes:

- Your fifty-word bio
- Additional topics that showcase your expertise

- Places, programs, podcasts, television, blogs, where you have been featured
- Links to previous interview videos
- Social media stats/reach
- Book titles and links
- Contact information
- Event Calendar Link if you have speaking or interview engagements and approve of your travel being public knowledge

Be clear about who is your target audience. Be concise in what you offer, and the topic you share while allowing your personality to show through. I cover personality knowledge in the hosting a podcast chapter.

You are now ready to guest on a podcast, radio, or television. Congratulations for taking your next best step. Keep reading to discover the best practices for hosting a podcast.

BEST PRACTICES

TO

HOST YOUR PODCAST

(((7)))

BEST HOSTING PRACTICE 1

Identify Your Podcasting Personality

Now that you know what it feels like to be in the interviewee seat, and you're still interested in the industry, you arc the perfect candidate to host your own podcast.

As in the section on being a guest, I recommend you walk through each of these eleven best practices in order. Resist the temptation to plow ahead. Missing one section will impact the outcome of you hosting a successful podcast.

Guesting on a podcast provides an opportunity to meet numerous personalities. In the process, you can see the persona differences are at times subtle and at times a force to be reckoned with. A best practice to help you excel as a guest and as a host is to identify how God designed you and to intentionally walk in the strengths of your design.

Walking in your strengths will enhance any podcast you guest on by helping you engage better with your host and to supply the listeners with practical applications they can receive with ease. Understanding the areas where you are not as strong and filling your gaps with virtual assistants or local talent who have that strength will help to grow your podcasting platform exponentially. When you speak with intentional awareness of the personalities, you will maximize your audience engagement to meet their needs on an intimate level.

My *LINKED® Quick Guides* coauthor, Linda Gilden, and I, spent years learning and teaching about personalities. Over time, we found a need to create a concise, yet relationally impactful assessment to help our coaching clients understand their natural design to better engage with those they loved and worked with. The *LINKED® Quick Guide to Personalities* is the first book in the series.

The original LINKED® book, along with *LINKED® for Educators*, *LINKED® for Parents*, and *LINKED® for*

Couples have won awards and are touted as "The first personality assessment I have taken that did not leave me bewildered and confused. Instead, it gave me the freedom I needed to be myself!" "A great resource for learning how to make the most of relationships, the communication that happens in them, and avoiding miscommunication."

Take a moment to discover *How God Designed You* through the twenty-six-question assessment found on my website LindaGoldfarb.com. In this section you are introduced to four distinct personalities: the get-it-done Mobilizer, the life-of-the-party Socializer, the keep-the-peace Stabilizer, and the everything-in-order Organizer.

Each of the four chapters provides you with three tendencies of the highlighted personality, the natural associated strength with each one, and how that strength could become a negative for you as a podcaster.

You will associate with one of these personalities or perhaps a blend of two or three. Taking the free assessment provides data to better assess your personality. Let's take a look at who you may be.

(((8)))

The Mobilizer-Leader

Are you a get-it-done Mobilizer?

You work best with people you respect.

Your natural ability to work quickly may cause you to miss details.

You have a knack for leadership.

As natural leaders, Mobilizers quickly push forward to complete tasks with excellence. This is a beneficial trait when we are only concerned with finishing a project or meeting a deadline. Yet, as podcasters we deal mostly with people. And we don't get far in building relationships if our highest concern is getting to the end of a project.

WHAT'S A MOBILIZER-LEADER TO DO?

To better engage with our listeners as Mobilizer podcast hosts it's best to consider how our natural communication practices may interfere with our desired results. Below are three tendencies we may encounter on a weekly basis and how we can handle them to benefit our listeners.

Mobilizer leaders tend to get angry when we lose control. Angry outbursts are a natural defense practice of Mobilizers. Think porcupine. When stressed the quills protrude and anyone coming into contact will be painfully punctured. To defuse our anger, it's best to re-evaluate the importance of controlling situations and, instead, give them over to the Lord or other capable hands.

Another tendency is to isolate when we're overwhelmed. A best practice to prevent this is to designate a smaller workload from the beginning. We can't be all things to all people. Start small and grow from there. Unachieved expectations quickly flow into self-doubt and shutting down for our get it done types.

The third tendency is to carry the bulk of the work on our own shoulders. A best practice to lighten our load is delegation. Define two or three duties not befitting your expertise or use of time. Perhaps allow someone else to contact potential guests. Hire out the designing of branded logos and promotional material.

Consider a cohost to help shoulder the load during a broadcast.

SURROUNDING OURSELVES WITH PEOPLE WE RESPECT AND TRUST, ADDS BREATHING ROOM IN OUR WEEK-TO-WEEK BUSINESS PRACTICES.

When you move forward, remember these three Mobilizer-Leader principles for success:

- Redefine what you must control
- Designate smaller workloads
- Hire people you trust

Step forward with confidence and trust God's design.

(((9)))

The Socializer-Talker

Are you a life-of-the-party Socializer?

You work best with people who enjoy your fun side.

Your natural ability to multi-task may cause you to get overwhelmed.

You have a knack for entertaining.

As natural talkers, Socializers eagerly engage others with enthusiasm and fun. This trait is fabulous when we have free reign to talk as long as we want without defined time limits. However, the life of a podcasting host usually involves timed segments and the need to focus on one subject at a time.

WHAT'S A SOCIALIZER-TALKER TO DO?

To better engage with our listeners as Socializer podcast hosts it's best to consider how our natural communication practices may interfere with our desired results. Below are three tendencies we may encounter on a weekly basis and how we can handle them to benefit our listeners.

As Socializer Talkers, one tendency is to base success on having fun. Discouragement comes into play when we stop having fun. Think Tigger from *Winnie the Pooh*. The wonderful thing about Tiggers is they enjoy fun. When life becomes a chore, Tigger shuts down. Discouragement becomes a time trap for Socializers. To forego discouragement, it's best to include fun as a portion of your podcast. Upbeat music, positive topics, and fun guests make hosting en-joy-able.

Another tendency is to want everyone to like us. The problem occurs when we correlate episode download numbers with listeners liking us as opposed to perhaps their dislike of the subject matter. A best practice to prevent dissatisfaction from happening is to poll our audience for the topics they would like us to cover. We can't be all things to all people, but we can give them what they want if we ask upfront.

The third tendency is very high highs and extremely low lows. A best practice to avoid quick burn out from drama trauma is to pace ourselves. Socializers move forward quickly, but often without planning. Additional help or a co-host will lessen the load on our shoulders. Thus, keeping us happy, happy in the process.

Surrounding ourselves with people who enjoy detail work and meeting deadlines helps ensure the completion of our week-to-week business practices. Saying yes to less helps us achieve more without feeling overwhelmed.

SAYING YES TO LESS HELPS US ACHIEVE MORE WITHOUT FEELING OVERWHELMED.

When you move forward remember these three Socializer-Talker principles for success:

- Include a fun element in the podcast
- Poll the audience and give them what they ask for
- Surround yourself with detail-oriented coworkers

Rejoice in God's design. He has you exactly where He needs you.

(((10)))

The Stabilizer-Peacekeeper

Are you a keep-the-peace Stabilizer?

You work best with people who don't try to control you.

Your natural ability to maintain calm under pressure may result in procrastination.

You have a knack for making everyone feel welcomed and included.

As natural peacekeepers, Stabilizers consistently seek to help others feel welcomed. Feeling relaxed with a podcasting host is a plus except when there's not a defined point to the episode. Audiences tune in to find content geared to moving forward in some area of life.

As a Stabilizer, plan to rest before and after an episode to maintain the joy you experience as a podcaster.

WHAT'S A STABILIZER-PEACEKEEPER TO DO?

To better engage with our listeners as Stabilizer podcast hosts it's best to consider how our natural communication practices may interfere with our desired results. Below are three tendencies we may encounter on a weekly basis and how we can handle them to benefit our listeners.

As Stabilizer Peacekeepers, one tendency is stubbornness when backed into a corner. Digging in our heals is a natural defensive practice of Stabilizers. Think donkey. When overburdened, or overtaxed, a donkey becomes immoveable. To prevent situations that get our back up, it's best to define the time requirements needed to make our job easy. Perhaps we begin with a twice a month broadcast and we make our episodes fifteen minutes in length. Minimum episode drops per month with shorter recorded timeframes makes our podcast concise and doable.

Another tendency is to produce a slow-paced program. A best practice to prevent this from happening is to be aware of how we interact with our listeners. Be prepared with thought provoking questions and answers that move the listener forward. We don't have to jump up and down during an episode, but we don't want the listeners to tune out. Find a middle ground pace, get to the point, and always give a call to action such as, "Join this conversation by sharing one tip in the comments that you use to..."

The third tendency is to disappear when life becomes chaotic. A best practice to reduce stress before it begins is to give ourselves achievable goals. Easy to reach goals could be, recording two episodes every other week or uploading two episodes to your platform every Thursday.

SHORT TERM GOALS WITH MEASURABLE RESULTS HELP US STAY FOCUSED.

When you move forward remember these three Stabilizer-Peacekeeper principles for success:

- Define time requirements
- Prepare thought provoking questions
- Create reachable short-term goals

Never mistake difference as a weakness. You are exactly how God designed you.

(((11)))

The Organizer-Thinker

Are you an everything-in-order Organizer?

You work best with people who follow the rules.

Your natural ability to look before you leap may cause you to procrastinate.

You have a knack for details.

As natural researchers, Organizers methodically uncover details to enhance projects with perfection. Statistics and deep insight bring depth and value to podcasting episodes except when that's all a listener hears. The degree of research can come across as boring or monotone to the listener and this is a tune-out factor that spells disaster.

WHAT'S AN ORGANIZER-THINKER TO DO?

To better engage with our listeners as Organizer podcast hosts it's best to consider how our natural communication practices may interfere with our desired results. Below are three tendencies we may encounter on a weekly basis and how we can handle them to benefit our listeners.

As Organizer Thinkers, one tendency is to pull back when others don't engage with us. The silent treatment is a natural defense for Organizers. Think mime. You can have a lot of great information but if you remain silent, no one will hear you. To ensure our voice is heard, we have to trust that what we say has value and speak out without waiting for an invitation.

Another tendency is to overwhelm our audience with too many details. A best practice to prevent losing your listeners is to include stories interspersed within your statistics or research. We enjoy helping others understand how to be their best. Yet coming across pushy in the process will turn off listeners.

The third tendency is to expect perfection from ourselves, which can result in procrastination. A best practice to let go and move forward is to define reasonable measures of success. Doing our best is always reachable when we define success. Delegating tasks with the understanding that another person's best, though different from ours, will get the job done releases our perfectionist mindset.

Overwhelm only occurs when our expectations run beyond our capacity to produce.

OVERWHELM ONLY OCCURS WHEN OUR EXPECTATIONS RUN BEYOND OUR CAPACITY TO PRODUCE.

When you move forward remember these three Organizer-Thinker principles for success:

- Trust in your value
- Include story with your research
- Let go of the perfectionist mindset

Your attention to detail is an enviable asset. God's design shines through perfectly.

One personality is not better than another and we may find ourselves as a blend of two or three. Understanding our foundational design is beneficial to hosting a successful podcast.

Now you know how God designed you, let's move on to the nuts and bolts of hosting your podcast. With the personality knowledge, you are one step closer to effectively presenting your knowledge, message, and ministry to your audience in a way they will understand.

(((12)))

BEST HOSTING PRACTICE 2

Choose Your Podcast Mission

The focused mission of a faith-based podcaster sets the tone of their show. In the following sections you will discover if this season is the best time to host a podcast.

When your decision to host a podcast is clear, your focus can then be scattered like seeds on good soil multiplying your reach in a variety of ways. Let's get going by addressing the deception of splattering verses scattering.

Faith-based writers work within genres. Though certain aspects of writing overlap from one genre to another, there are much needed guidelines distinct to the type of book. The differing guidelines strengthen our content to be best understood by the reader.

The Scattered verses Splattered Guidelines help you discover and focus on your next best step professionally and personally.

This discovery tool helps you determine if podcasting is your next best step. Will podcasting splatter your mission or scatter it into the reach of more reading listeners.

A SPLATTERED MISSION

Think of paint splattered on a wall. In the center of the wall is a large splat of your favorite color paint.

To help you visualize this concept, write your favorite color here:

Now envision splashes and splats of differing colors thrown haphazardly on the same wall. Can you see the picture? Some of the colors may connect with your core color, while others are off by themselves. They're on the same wall, your wall, but they have no intersecting relationship with your favorite color. Some of the colors may even clash horribly with our favorite color, yet they're still on our wall.

When we experience a splattered mission, our life is reflective of this wall. Chaos. Though the wall may be colorful, there is no rhyme or reason as to why we have given the splats space in our life. Confusion and procrastination set in, quickly followed by shutdown.

Our Lord designed us on purpose, for His purpose. In the process, He set us apart with spiritual gifts and personalities to be the best we can to accomplish His desire for our lives. And living splattered with lack of order is not God's best for us.

Instead of having a wall splattered with options and opportunities that may lead us away from His best use, we can visualize a core mission, that is utilized in multiple ways to benefit His kingdom.

I call this a Scattered Mission.

A SCATTERED MISSION

Think of scattering seeds. When you are focused on one mission, you can extend your impact, engage with your audience beyond the book, and equip your audience by scattering the seeds of your knowledge among a variety of platforms—podcasting being one of them.

No matter how we spend them, there are only twenty-four hours in a day. Yet, I've found by focusing on our faith and family first, we wind up with quality time left over to invest in our next best step.

How much time do you spend nurturing your faith and family each week? Write out your daily activity for each. An example would be: Thirty minutes each morning in Bible study. Thirty minutes journaling my prayers. One hour preparing meals for my children.

Carpooling the kids to school. Caregiving for my parents. The purpose of this exercise is to determine your time availability to successfully feed into podcasting without disrupting your current spiritual and relational habits.

Faith:____

____

Family:______________________________________

____

If you work outside the home add the number of hours required daily.

Job:____

____

I intentionally view my life as a whole. By not separating my spiritual, relational, and professional aspects of who I am, I have a realistic understanding of my next best step. Three areas I consider beyond faith, family, and job are time, finances, and calling.

I have a link to access a downloadable mind map diagram in the Resources.

WHERE WE EFFECTIVELY SPEND OUR TIME DETERMINES THE OUTCOME OF OUR SUCCESS.

Time. How much free time do you have each week to invest in podcasting? Be realistic and mark on your calendar when you would begin and end each day.

Finances. How much spendable income do you have to invest in podcasting. There are monthly fees for hosting a podcast, recording software investment, and recording equipment.

Calling. How will your podcast fit into God's calling on your life? As a writer, you have a genre focus. Will this podcast utilize your current content, or do you need to create new content?

Consider the twenty-four hours you have every day, 168-hours per week, and decide if there's room for podcasting without compromising your faith and family obligations.

If you agree that podcasting is your next best step in this season, consider which of these four missions fit you best: to educate, entertain, equip, or evangelize.

(((13)))

Mission Choices

Is Education Your Mission?

Education is defined as information about or training in a particular field or subject. If you desire to fill the minds of your listeners with knowledge and to help them grow in a certain area of life, education could be your mission.

While you develop your podcast episodes include a teaching. Perhaps develop a course on your subject that listeners can buy based on what you give during your podcast.

IS ENTERTAINMENT YOUR MISSION?

Entertainment is defined as the action of providing others with amusement or enjoyment. If you desire to make people laugh, or to take life a little less seriously, this may be the mission for you.

As an entertainer, you are not as interested in the takeaway of your episode as much as you are the break from the hustle and bustle for your listeners. Be sure to include age-appropriate humor and possibly a YouTube page for your audience to see you as much as they listen to you.

IS EQUIPPING YOUR MISSION?

Equipping is defined as preparing someone mentally for a particular situation or task. If you desire to help your listeners achieve more in life, then equipping may be your mission.

Counseling or coaching is a great fit for this category. Providing an online interactive monthly group coaching through Zoom would be a great extension of your platform.

IS EVANGELISM YOUR MISSION?

Evangelism is defined as the spreading of the Christian gospel by public preaching or personal witness. If you desire your listeners to grow in their faith, evangelism may be your best choice.

Bible study and devotional content work great in this category. Consider creating weekly or monthly Scripture memorization PDF downloads available on your website to include in your show notes.

Based on the four mission options, how would you define your mission? Is it a single focus or a blend? The right answer is whatever you choose. The key is to make a choice and stick with it for at least six to twelve months.

List your thoughts here:

(((14)))

BEST HOSTING PRACTICE 3

Choose Your Podcast Format

Podcasters vary, and like discovering your favorite coffee or tea flavor, your best choice of formats may take some practice runs. The beautiful thing about hosting your program is that it's yours.

You want to consider the category where your podcast fits best on the podcasting platforms. According to popular vote from several online sources, the five podcast categories with highest traffic in 2023 were: society and culture, religion and spirituality, education, business and technology, and health and fitness.

Search online for current podcasting categories and write in the top three that fit your program:

First choice:______________________________

Second choice:_____________________________

Third choice:______________________________

When you've selected your categories, look at the following format options and decide where you feel the best equipped to begin. The format you easily gravitate to may be your best fit, right now. As you grow your podcast, be flexible to consider blending one or two formats until you find the fit that draws in your audience.

Make notes under each format that fits your podcast mission.

CONVERSATIONAL PODCASTS

Think of a living room setting or perhaps a kitchen table with coffee or tea served with conversation about everyday topics. Based on your current writing topic/genre, what three topics would be your focus in a conversational setting?

TOPIC 1:______________________________

TOPIC 2:______________________________

TOPIC 3:______________________________

INTERVIEW PODCASTS

Think of meeting your favorite author, actor, or successful businessperson and getting answers to questions with no interruptions.

Based on your current writing topic/genre, what three topics would be your focus in an interview setting?

TOPIC 1: ____________________

TOPIC 2: ____________________

TOPIC 3: ____________________

INVESTIGATIVE PODCASTS

Think of your favorite news anchor who shares breaking news with enthusiasm and an unbiased opinion about a hot topic.

Based on your current writing topic/genre, what three topics would be your focus in an investigative setting?

TOPIC 1: ____________________

TOPIC 2: ____________________

TOPIC 3: ____________________

MONOLOGUE PODCASTS

Think of a solo opinion-based program with how-to or general living practical application.

Based on your current writing topic/genre, what three topics, if any, would be your focus in a monologue setting?

TOPIC 1: ____________________

TOPIC 2: ____________________

TOPIC 3: ____________________

ROUNDTABLE PODCASTS

Think of a panel of experts or communicators coming together to share beneficial insights with enthusiasm on a particular subject.

Based on your current writing topic/genre, what three topics would be your focus in a roundtable setting?

TOPIC 1:____________________________________

TOPIC 2:____________________________________

TOPIC 3:____________________________________

Who would you have in the roundtable with you?

STORYTELLING PODCASTS

Think of an audiobook narrator who shares your favorite series of books or poetry. Or perhaps you could read children stories aloud.

Based on your current writing topic/genre, what three topics would be your focus in a storytelling setting?

TOPIC 1:____________________________________

TOPIC 2:____________________________________

TOPIC 3:____________________________________

THEATRICAL PODCASTS

Think of multiple actors performing together with sound effects and a musical interlude.

Based on your current writing topic/genre, what three topics would be your focus in a theatrical setting?

TOPIC 1:____________________________
TOPIC 2:____________________________
TOPIC 3:____________________________

HYBRID PODCASTS

Think of a combination of any of the above-mentioned formats presented with excellence.

For instance. In a 60-minute episode, maybe do a monologue for 20 minutes, have a guest for 20 minutes, and storytelling or return to your monologue for 20 minutes.

Based on your current writing topic/genre, what three topics would be your focus and what combination of settings would you choose?

TOPIC 1:____________________________
TOPIC 2:____________________________
TOPIC 3:____________________________

Based on the formats mentioned, which is your best fit? If you are ready to commit to starting a podcast, fill in the blank below:

I will commit to the____________________ ________________format for a minimum of six months.

Now, let's name your podcast.

(((15)))

BEST HOSTING PRACTICE 4

Choose Your Podcast Name

What's in a name? Everything!

Before you make one of the most important strategic choices a podcaster has to make, let's recap what you've discovered to this point. Write the decisions you've made for each category.

Your dominant or blended podcasting personality:

Your audience:

Your mission:

Your format:

The perfect name for your show should convey the feel of all four answers combined, not three out of four. *All. Four.* Matching all four tightens your focus. The more succinct you are in combining all four, the less likely you are to become dissatisfied with your title.

Staying Real About Faith & Family offers weekly episodes and fits my Mobilizer/Socializer personality blend while I help families strengthen their faith and have fun doing it. My audience is families of faith. My mission is to equip/entertain/evangelize people of faith, and my co-hosted format is a hybrid of conversational/interview. I offer weekly released solo episodes of *Let's Journey Together, a Moment with Father* as secondary devotion-based episodes under the *Staying Real* umbrella. *Let's Journey Together* drops Monday, Wednesday, and Friday with the mission of storytelling and evangelizing.

Your Best Writing Life fits my Mobilizer/Socializer style to help writers get their projects done and have fun in the process. My audience is Christian writers. My mission is educating/equipping writers in a conversational/interview format.

You'll notice the number of words in each podcast title ranges from four to six. Generally, use one word (your tagline must be spot on to support a one-word title) or more, but less than ten.

Now it's your turn, fill in the blanks:

______________________________________fits my

________________________________personality style.

My audience is ______________________________,

my mission is to ____________________________,

and my format is ____________________________.

You may want to brainstorm your top three ideas with individuals who represent your listeners. Let them know your personality, mission, and the format you have chosen. All three are key factors for branding purposes.

With your title in place, it's time to describe your podcast.

Write Your Podcast Description

Your podcast description, located in your podcasting platform page, helps listeners discover more details about you, your content, and your posting schedule. If you include interviews, list the email address and submission guidelines to help potential guests provide the information you will use to decide if they are a fit.

Two examples:

Your Best Writing Life

Each Tuesday, Linda Goldfarb and her writing industry experts share content for all levels of writers. You receive practical information and how-to applications to grow your writing career as a faith-based author.

We provide content to help you grow as a Christian writer to make your next book proposal, manuscript editing, speaking event, and writer's conference worth your time and energy.

Our episodes average 30-45 minutes.

Hit subscribe and join our family of writers.

Your Best Writing Life is associated with the Blue Ridge Mountains Christian Writers Conference.

To request a guest interview intake sheet, email Heather.YourBestWritingLife@gmail.com

Staying Real About Faith & Family

Inspiration with practical application to help Christian families hold on to their faith as they navigate real-life issues. *Staying Real About Faith & Family* drops each Saturday with Board-Certified Christian Life Coach Linda Goldfarb and co-host Heather Greer in the drivers' seats. Linda's enthusiasm and insight, along with Heather's balancing practical banter, and their guests' inspiring stories, plus your desire to grow spiritually and relationally, is the path to healthier relationships between you and God and those you love. Bonus devotionals with Linda are sprinkled throughout the week to encourage and inspire your faith walk. To request a guest interview intake sheet, send an inquiry to Heather at StayingRealAboutFaithandFamily@gmail.com

Podcast descriptions vary based on the category and mission of the hosts. Be sure you find a sweet balance between too much info that no one will read and not enough to get them interested. On average, fifty to one hundred fifty words is sufficient.

It's Your Turn to Write a Podcast Description

Now it's time for you to give it a try. Be aware that you may find yourself honing the description over the course of time. Periodically, review and update the description to insure your content continues to match who you say you are.

Start by compiling the necessary elements.

Title:______________________________

Name of host(s):_______________________

Day your episodes drop or release: (It is common to record shows ahead of time to upload and schedule. The day and time you select for each episode to become available to listeners is when they *drop*.)_____

____

Average length of the episodes:______________

Summary of your content: (Use a broad-brush concept here.)___________________________

Names of sponsors, if any:__________________

Compile your info and write the description below. Be sure your voice shines through. The tone of a podcast is heard in the description._______________

____

____

When your description is set, you can script your podcast trailer. Listen to several examples in your format to get a feel for what might work best for your podcast.

Create Your Podcast Trailer

An audio trailer runs two to five minutes. Generally, 700 words usually results in five minutes, depending on your recording pace. The pace can be motivated by the background music you use and enhanced by the person reading it.

Background or music bed audio can be found in several online locations, such as Pixabay, Soundcloud, and YouTube Audio Library.

Most music requires a license for commercial use, even copyright-free music. Be sure to read the terms of use before using an audio track.

Two examples of podcast trailers:

Example 1. Welcome to *Your Best Writing Life.* I'm your host, Linda Goldfarb. If you're looking for a podcast that offers easy to follow writing applications with practical information you can use right away, then *Your Best Writing Life* is your podcast. During our weekly episodes, you'll learn skills and strategies from industry experts, best-selling authors, editors, agents, bloggers, and podcasters, who share their best tips about the writing craft in general, self-care for writers, nonfiction writing tips, fiction writing tips, and the business of writing for all levels of writers from beginners to best sellers. *Your Best Writing Life* was founded by DiAnn Mills and Edie Melson, two storytellers who encourage writers to follow God, embrace excellence, and write boldly. Find out more about DiAnn and Edie in our show notes. Well, there you go. Ready to break through the obstacles holding you back from becoming the best writer you can be? Then, take just a moment and click subscribe. We're here to help you experience your best writing life and we don't want you to miss a thing. This is Linda Goldfarb, and I look forward to being here with you each week as you journey into *your best writing life*.

Example 2. Do you wonder why your Christian life is filled with struggles? While the person sitting next to you in church seems to have it all together? Is social media casting a false light that's stealing your joy? Maybe you're thinking about attending church yet fear your sins will be found out, and you'll be shunned. Let's get real folks. The majority of people who claim to be Christians know less about the God of Abraham, Isaac, and Jacob, than they do the fake lives of friends on social media. No one is perfect. No family is perfect. No community is perfect. And none of us have a promise from God that life will be perfect. Here's truth. Every God fearing, Jesus loving, Holy Spirit seeking Christian struggles. We struggle to find answers about marriages with differing spiritual beliefs, relational communication, parenting and family issues, respect for spiritual leadership, gender, church conflicts, helping our children navigate difficult situations, caregiving attitudes, and the list goes on. Whoa, it's more than enough to make your head hurt. So, if you're ready to get real without resistance, you're in the right place. I'm Linda Goldfarb, a sister in Christ, who has lived a lot of life with probably more years behind me than I have ahead of me. I don't claim to have answers beyond my life experiences, Father's truth, Messiah's sacrifice, and Holy Spirit's leading. And this my friend is *Staying Real About Faith and Family*. Each week I'll get real about relational topics challenging the hearts of believers. We'll see what Scripture reveals. Consider practical applications and ways we can walk out Kingdom living this side of glory, with less fear, less conflict, and less anxiety. I can't wait to meet you as we travel the narrow road together, *staying real about faith and family*.

You'll notice I announce my name quickly in the first example and midway in example two. This is personal preference, so use what feels right to you.

The podcast trailer is usually loaded into your podcasting platform first. Uploading your aforementioned trailer as your first release is a quick way to help listeners find you. When your trailer is loaded to your platform, you can begin the process of registering your podcast for distribution on additional platforms. For example, my podcasts are hosted on Buzzsprout,[5] yet they can be heard on numerous podcasting platforms, or directories, such as Apple Podcast, Spotify, and Google. Check with your podcast hosting service and review their process for adding your content to other directories.

Quick note, you may read recommendations to upload several episodes at one time verses the trailer first. This is personal preference. Apple podcast is a high-profile platform and for this reason, I waited until my trailer was visible on Apple before releasing additional episodes. I highly recommend having several episodes recorded, loaded to your podcasting platform, and lined up for future release.

It's time to move into branding your podcast.

(((16)))

BEST HOSTING PRACTICE 5

Choose Your Podcast Brand

Branding your podcast with purpose turns listeners into subscribers. Speak the language of your subscribers to draw them into conversation. No matter your formatting choice, every podcast episode flies or dies based on conversation.

Consider the three audiences you defined in Best Guesting Practice 2. In that chapter, you clarified the top needs of your audiences. Let's begin speaking the language of your subscribers based on your answers for only one need. As an example, I'll use a personality-based topic appropriate for my *Staying Real About Faith & Family* podcast.

SPEAK THE LANGUAGE OF YOUR SUBSCRIBERS

One need of many families is to have better communication skills for their relationships to thrive.

I fill the need for better communication by offering families a personality assessment to identify who's living under their roof and three strategies to better connect with each personality.

NO MATTER YOUR FORMATTING CHOICE, EVERY PODCAST EPISODE FLIES OR DIES BASED ON CONVERSATION.

I speak the language of my listeners by having transparent conversations with them. Since podcast episodes are recorded, you're not engaging in a live dialogue with your audience, yet your style should be such that they feel you are. I share the ups and downs that have occurred in my own family. These are transparency points I use while I share the strategies. Offering relatable conversation shows I'm a safe and trustworthy source. I'm willing to be honest, not perfect. I invite my audience to join the conversation by commenting on my episodes via my website or social media outlets.

Before writing the topics of your podcast, please become familiar with what you are willing to share with your listeners to connect with them on a transparent level as you take them on a journey of encouragement, entertainment, healing, discovery, and salvation.

List ways you can speak the language of your listeners here: ____

____

____

____

PINPOINT YOUR PRACTICAL TAGLINES

Taglines set your brand—along with confirming realistic expectations for subscribers. Choose your podcast tagline with a broad brush of practicality to allow for numerous topics within your niche.

For *Staying Real about Faith & Family*, this is my tagline: *Helping Christian families hold on to their faith as they navigate real-life issues*. Simple and to the point. With this tagline, you know who my audience is and the purpose of the show. The description does not limit my conversations.

Another example is *Your Best Writing Life–Practical information with how-to application to grow your writing career as a faith-based author*. By keeping the tagline practical, there's no second-guessing for our audiences. The listener is clear about what they will receive when listening to the podcast.

Give it a shot! Write in a few taglines to consider:

____

____

____

CREATE SHOW AND EPISODE ARTWORK

The visual effectiveness of your logo either breaks through the competition's lack of fortitude or your artwork sinks to the bottom of the podcasting pool. You want yours to break through the competition.

Follow these basic guidelines when creating a logo:

- 1800 x 1800 dimensions allows for details to show no matter the size required for marketing
- Frame your logo to ensure nothing is lost on a white background
- The host's photo is not required, but including one invites personal connection
- Create a show logo that remains static in the description
- Create an additional logo that matches your brand and offers additional information specific to each episode

Take the time to look at some podcast logos and their artwork. Check out the podcast logo and episode logos for *Your Best Writing Life* on your favorite podcasting platform or at this link https://www.blueridgeconference.com/podcast.

Search for additional logos in your category and by popularity. High profile celebrities usually host the top podcasts. Don't let popularity and positioning discourage you. Celebrity is not the goal here, getting your podcast listed for others to find is.

List your top podcast logo choices here along with why you liked them:________________________

____

____

____

Choose three to five people to check out the top three logos you like. Which do others prefer? Write the top selected choice below: __________________

____

____

____

Consider this top choice when designing your logo and other artwork.

You can certainly hire someone to create your logo, or you can try out Canva.com. Either way the info you have here is needed for the process.

(((17)))

BEST HOSTING PRACTICE 6

Create Your Podcast Content

Five broad-brush categories can expand into one year of podcast episodes. When you tie each category to your mission and purpose you can easily expand the content. Depending on the length and release schedule of your episodes, you can fill a year with quality programming.

Let's take a look at the award-winning *Your Best Writing Life* podcast for examples. You'll notice each category, fiction, nonfiction, marketing, soul care, and networking, is broad which allows me to offer several thirty-minute episode topics under each one. Each episode topic can be further expanded into part 1 and part 2, a series of three or more in addition to one-off topics.

CATEGORY ONE: FICTION

TOPIC 1: Create Characters Your Readers Will Love
Subtopic: Developing Whimsical Characters
Subtopic: Five Personality Quirks to Enhance Your Character

TOPIC 2: How to Plot Like a Pro
Subtopic: Three Plotting Techniques to Write Quickly

TOPIC 3: Develop Protagonists Your Readers Remember
Subtopic: Choose Your Protagonist's Best Name

TOPIC 4: Setting Your Scenes Up for Success
Subtopic: Three Scene Elements to Include in Every Mystery

TOPIC 5: World Building
Subtopic: The Top Three Ways to Map Your World

CATEGORY TWO: NONFICTION

TOPIC 1: Write Nonfiction with Fiction Elements
Subtopic: Five Ways to Bring Nonfiction to Life
Subtopic: Three Fiction Elements to Enhance How-To Books

TOPIC 2: Write Articles That Inspire

Subtopic: Write Articles for Young Adults in Three Steps

TOPIC 3: Addressing Sensitive Topics in Your Writing

Subtopic: Writing on Pornography for the Christian Market

TOPIC 4: What Qualifies a Book as Nonfiction

Subtopic: Top Selling Christian Nonfiction in 2024

TOPIC 5: Incorporating Story to Draw Readers to Your Nonfiction.

Subtopic: How Much Storytelling is Too Much in Nonfiction?

CATEGORY THREE: MARKETING

TOPIC 1: Create Effective Email Marketing Skills

Subtopic: The Top Email Marketing Platforms for 2024

TOPIC 2: How Mastermind Groups Increase Book Sales

Subtopic: Who to Include in a Mastermind Group

TOPIC 3: Take Advantage of Your Resource Table

Subtopic: Five Essentials for a Writer's Resource Table

TOPIC 4: Marketing on Social Media

Subtopic: Choose Your Top Three Social Media Platforms

TOPIC 5: The Most Effective Book Launching Protocols

Subtopic: Launching a Self-published Book

CATEGORY FOUR: SOUL CARE

TOPIC 1: The Purpose of Resting for Writers
Subtopic: How Do Different Personalities Rest?

TOPIC 2: Spiritual Foundations for Christian Writers
Subtopic: How to Balance a Writer's Prayer Life

TOPIC 3: Developing a Personal Prayer Team
Subtopic: Who Makes Your Best Prayer Partner

TOPIC 4: How to Experience a Spiritual Retreat Between Writing Projects
Subtopic: Top Tips to Help Writers Relax

TOPIC 5: How to Feed the Soul of a Writer
Subtopic: Three Weekly Gifts to Give Yourself

CATEGORY FIVE: NETWORKING

TOPIC 1: How to Create a YouTube Following
Subtopic: Create Effective YouTube Playlists

TOPIC 2: Why Attend Christian Writers Conferences?
Subtopic: Create a One-Year Writers Conference Journal

TOPIC 3: Create a Passionate Group of Social Media Followers
Subtopic: What Social Media Platform is Your Best Fit?

TOPIC 4: How to Start a Writers Critique Group
Subtopic: The Makings of an Effective Writer's Group

TOPIC 5: **Discover Local Networking Opportunities**
Subtopic: The Top Recommended Tools for Networking

Fifty-two episodes from five categories. Now it's your turn. Write in your categories first, and remember to think with a broad-brush mindset. Next, add your topics, then subtopics. Be aware that these are sample topics. Your guests may have different ideas that fit within your five categories. You can ask for specific topics from your guests in your intake sheet or ask them to speak on topics you need covered.

CATEGORY ONE:__________________________

TOPIC 1:________________________________

Subtopic:_______________________________

TOPIC 2:________________________________

Subtopic:_______________________________

TOPIC 3:________________________________

Subtopic:_______________________________

TOPIC 4:________________________________

Subtopic:_______________________________

TOPIC 5:________________________________

Subtopic:_______________________________

CATEGORY TWO: ______________________________

TOPIC 1: ______________________________

Subtopic: ______________________________

TOPIC 2: ______________________________

Subtopic: ______________________________

Topic 3: ______________________________

Subtopic: ______________________________

TOPIC 4: ______________________________

Subtopic: ______________________________

TOPIC 5: ______________________________

Subtopic: ______________________________

CATEGORY THREE: ______________________________

TOPIC 1: ______________________________

Subtopic: ______________________________

TOPIC 2: ______________________________

Subtopic: ______________________________

TOPIC 3: ______________________________

Subtopic: ______________________________

TOPIC 4: ______________________________

Subtopic: ______________________________

TOPIC 5: ______________________________

Subtopic: ______________________________

CATEGORY FOUR: ______________________________

TOPIC 1: ______________________________

Subtopic:______________________________

TOPIC 2:______________________________

Subtopic:______________________________

TOPIC 3:______________________________

Subtopic:______________________________

TOPIC 4:______________________________

Subtopic:______________________________

TOPIC 5:______________________________

Subtopic:______________________________

CATEGORY FIVE:_________________________

TOPIC 1:______________________________

Subtopic:______________________________

TOPIC 2:______________________________

Subtopic:______________________________

TOPIC 3:______________________________

Subtopic:______________________________

TOPIC 4:______________________________

Subtopic:______________________________

TOPIC 5:______________________________

Subtopic:______________________________

EFFECTIVE EPISODE OUTLINES

An effective episode outline is one that fits your style and meets the expectations of your subscribers. All podcast episodes have essential elements and preferential elements. We look at both in this section.

It's good to note that whether your episodes drop once a week or once a month, consistency builds your subscriber base. The same works for your episode outline. Consistency is key. That said, it may take a couple months to discover the flow that works best for you and your subscribers. Don't get discouraged, stay determined to find your best fit.

I use Buzzsprout for my podcasting platform. It offers several free show guidelines and numerous tutorials that I recommend. You are given the space to write in the duration of each segment to keep track of your time. Here is one basic example I use for a thirty-minute show:

Cold intro. Pose a question or two as a teaser for the episode content. (Thirty to thirty-five seconds)

Segue. Consider something like "Don't go away, Staying Real About Faith & Family begins… right now!"

[Music or jingle begins] Search online for copyright free music for podcasts.

Intro. Length can range from ten to ninety seconds: (__) [Set the stage for your episode. Include details that set up your episode's theme. State name of podcast show, why your show exists, and who you are]

See examples below of the intros I use for my two podcasts.

"Hello and/or welcome to [podcast title], the show that [insert concept of show or tagline]. I'm [host name]. In today's episode, we will discuss [insert talking points] with [guest name]. We'll share the ins and outs of [episode topic] and offer you a special surprise at the end. Be sure to listen all the way through for the details!"
Today's guest is [full name of guest]. [First name of guest] is… [give short bio]
[Banter with guest] We're so happy to have you join our conversation as we discuss [show topic] Welcome [guests name] to [name of show].

Guest responds

Segue into the episode topic with a summary of the points you'll share. Open the show.

Topic or Question 1: Insert your desired timeframe, five minutes, ten minutes, to help you stay on track: (___)

1. Main point______________________________
2. Additional data___________________________
3. Reinforcing quote

[**Segue**] Banter and connect the first point to the second.

Topic or Question 2: Timeframe:(___)

1. Main point

2. Additional data
3. Reinforcing quote

Topic or Question 3: Timeframe:(___)

1. Main point
2. Additional data
3. Reinforcing quote

Soft Close: Summarize the main points you covered, tease an upcoming episode, or a special event.

Thank guest. Include contact info in the show notes.

Call to action: Subscribe, leave comments on our website, invite a friend to listen in.

Closing remark: Create a memorable statement to be used at the end of every episode. See examples below.

[Closing music jingle or sound effect can begin with your call to action then fades after your last closing remark.]

Here are the two opening/intro examples from my podcasts spoken after the cold intros:

Your Best Writing Life: "Welcome to *Your Best Writing Life*, an extension of the Blue Ridge Mountains Christian Writers Conference held in the beautiful Blue Ridge Mts of North Carolina. I'm your host Linda Goldfarb. Each week I bring tips and strategies from writing and publishing industry experts to help you excel in your craft. I'm so glad you're listening in."

Staying Real about Faith & Family: "Welcome to *Staying Real About Faith & Family.* If you're looking for a community where you can get real about life without resistance, you're in the right place. I'm Linda Goldfarb. Each week, Heather Greer and I, along with our guests, offer personal insight to encourage transparent living from a biblical viewpoint with practical applications. Staying real with Holy Spirit's leading is what we're all about. We pray today's episode blesses you."

Here are the two closing examples from my two podcasts:

Your Best Writing Life: "Thank you, friends for joining us. Please take a moment to share this podcast with another writer or two, give us a star rating, post a episode review, and hit subscribe. I greatly appreciate what you have to say as much as what you choose to write. This is Linda Goldfarb and I look forward to being with you next time on *Your Best Writing Life*."

Staying Real About Faith & Family: "May YHWH bless you and keep you in all you do. Until next time, this is Linda Goldfarb, and Heather, *staying real about faith and family*."

EVERYONE CAN USE A LITTLE PROMPTING

In addition to the obvious episode themes or topics best fitting your expertise, take a moment to consider the following creative prompt ideas.

THEME PROMPTS

Seasonal Food Topics. Use Winter, Spring, Summer, and Fall themes and incorporate recipes.

Quarterly Topics. January-March, April-June, July-September, and October-December

National/International Holidays. Christmas, Easter, Biblical Feasts.

Check out https://www.timeanddate.com/holidays for additional holidays.

Day of Topics. National Day of Prayer.

Check out https://www.daysoftheyear.com

Write in topics specific to your podcast:___________

(((18)))

BEST HOSTING PRACTICE 7

Create Your Podcast Guest Interview Sheet

Interviewing people who best fit your mission and promises made to your audience via your title, will guarantee a quality episode. An interview intake sheet helps you weed out those who are not a good fit. Here's what I include in my guest intake sheet for *Your Best Writing Life*. Modify this format to fit your podcast needs.

Insert show logo on the left side of sheet.

Include in the header: Podcast Title, Interview Intake sheet, Length of program.

Length of recording time. Episodes run approximately thirty minutes, but I have guests on with me for forty-five minutes to cover pre and post episode details and email of host or booking personnel for your podcast.

Requested personal information from guest: Guest name, mailing address, cell phone, and email.

Directions for guest to email completed form to your designated email. What interview categories fit your expertise? Mark all that apply:

- Writing Craft
- Speaking Craft
- Writer/speaker Soul Care
- Specialties: Such as The Writer's Personality, Brain Science and Writers, Marketing, Book Launches, and Social Media

List in order of preference the topics you're qualified to talk about that benefit our audience of faith and family.

Provide two or three interview questions/talking points for your number one topic.

If your topic fits our need, you will be notified by email and given recording dates to choose from.

As a guest on Your Best Writing Life, we ask that you rate and review our show on your favorite podcasting platform and publicize your episode on social media.

Fifty-word bio to introduce you.

Provide social media, website, book links for our show notes.

Do you have a book/resource/event you'd like us to focus on at the end of the interview? If yes, what is the name and where can the audience go for this resource. (Amazon, bookstore, your website.)

Are you willing to supply a downloadable give-away to listeners we can post a link to in our show notes? If yes, please provide the link once your topic is selected.

Please attach a high definition headshot to the return email for publicity purposes. Do not embed the photo in this sheet.

Additional information you want Linda to know prior to your interview.

I give Linda Goldfarb permission to use my interview for show publicity/marketing.

Signature: ________________________________

Date ________________________________

19

BEST HOSTING PRACTICE 8

Choose Your Podcast Hosting Service

A Podcast Hosting Service (PHS) is where you store your media files, and where they will be distributed to your listeners. These services usually provide features like single or multiple episode embeddable media players, a website on their platform, podcast analytics of who's listening, where they are listening from, and what devices they are listening through. You can upload your audio files to your website, but if you seek an optimized and efficient way to reach more listeners, Podcast Hosting Services are the way to go.

In this section, learn what to look for in a PHS, and I'll share some of the top Podcast Hosting Services available at this printing.

WHAT PODCAST HOSTING SERVICES SHOULD PROVIDE

All PHS are different, and you get what you pay for. That said, you should expect your platform to offer the following.

Storage. This is the online location where your mp3 audio episodes are uploaded for distribution.

Accessibility. This is the ease at which listeners can locate and listen to your podcast.

Analytics. These are the statistics and data pertaining to your episode.

Monetization Options. These are options suggested to bring in money for your episodes.

TOP PODCAST HOSTING SERVICES

Podcast hosting services range from free to premium cost-wise. Base your PHS selection on your budget and your dedication to hosting your podcast for at least six months. With a six-month commitment you are more apt to invest in your podcasting as a career not a hobby. A future endeavor that's part of your bigger plan does. Keep this in mind as you check out the platforms listed below. Disclaimer: I'm listing these sites, but I have not vetted them for anything other than their ranking in the industry.

Many PHS offer free hosting for beginners. If you are personally committing to a minimum of six months, you may outgrow the features of the free hosting. I'm not saying don't try the no cost route, just remember these services are free for a reason.

I currently use Buzzsprout for both of my podcasts. Buzzsprout offers a free entry level hosting program and premium hosting. I pay a monthly fee for my hosting and find the service to be user-friendly and worth the investment as one of the top recommended sites.

The top eleven podcast hosting sites as of this printing are:

1. Buzzsprout
2. Podbean
3. Blubrry
4. Libsyn
5. Spreaker
6. Anchor
7. Captivate
8. Transistor
9. Simplecast
10. Soundcloud
11. Podomatic

Set aside a couple hours to check out each of these sites. Ask for recommendations from current podcasters.

Weigh the pros and cons to find your best fit. Keep your mission and audience in mind.

WHICH PODCAST HOSTING SERVICES WILL YOU USE?

List your top three choices and the pros and cons of each.

PHS 1:________________________________

____

____

____

PHS 2:________________________________

____

____

____

PSH 3:________________________________

____

____

____

When you've chosen your podcasting platform, it's time to choose the best equipment for your budget.

(((20)))

BEST HOSTING PRACTICE 9

Choose Podcast Editing and Recording Equipment

Podcasting equipment is not created equal, and the key to being taken seriously as a podcaster is editing each episode.

Dead air. Numerous umms. Loud floor noise. These three distractions alone can quickly give listeners reason to stop tuning in.

Depending on the software you choose, you'll have numerous tutorial options. Use these tutorials. Become the best editor of your episodes or hire someone to do this step. Following all the previous best practices and foregoing this one will prove disastrous. Excellent editing results in a professional quality podcast.

AUDIO EDITING SOFTWARE

Audacity is a free resource available for PC and Mac, but Adobe Audition is the software I use.

A number of audio editing software options are available for every budget. As with choosing a podcasting host, I recommend researching editing software options to determine the best fit for your budget and abilities. Search Google for the most up-to-date list of podcasting software.

ONLINE RECORDING OPTIONS

SquadCast is getting rave reviews. It offers a reliable podcast recording experience, ensuring quality, speed, and reliability with every recording session. The use of "progressive uploads allow you to encode media sources into chunks, which are uploaded to the cloud while recording instead of after you click Stop."

Zencastr is the online studio I currently use to record my guest interview episodes and solo episodes. Zencastr provides postproduction services that provide clean audio and video which can be uploaded directly to my podcasting platform. I usually apply a few more postproduction tweaks to satisfy my personal preferences.

To find additional online recording services search for 'online podcast recording services.'

RECORDING EQUIPMENT

I suggest a USB microphone to plug directly into your computer or laptop. Search 'podcasting USB microphone' for your options. As always, you get the quality you pay for.

I use a red set of Samson headphones when I record to keep outside noise from distracting me and to ensure there's no feedback during the recording when I interview my guests. I mention the color because it matches my personality. The best headphones are the ones you use consistently and that offer a bit of comfort to your ears in the process. An uncomfortable set of headphones is not worth the pennies you paid for it.

Laptop or computer? I'm a Mac girl. I own the best MacBook Pro I can afford. Many successful podcasters use a PC. This is a business, and you need quality equipment you can depend on, so choose wisely.

External drives are fabulous additions to store your audio files. Search 'external drives' for whatever type of computer you use. Choose the best option your budget allows. Backup your episodes to the drive weekly or save directly to your external drive.

Podcasting is a personal adventure. With that in mind, sitting under the mentorship of those who have gone before you is priceless. The next three chapters include the answers from veteran podcasters to frequently asked questions to empower your new adventure and get you started off on the right foot.

(((21)))

BEST HOSTING PRACTICE 10

Always Be Teachable

I polled a diverse sampling of active podcasters to provide you with answers to the top three questions new podcasters need to address early in their careers.

- How do I make sure I am providing quality content?
- What can I do to help people return for more episodes?
- How do I prevent personally burning out?

Question 1

How do I make sure I am providing quality content?

"Quality content is share-worthy content. Your listeners will recommend the episodes they find valuable. Provide the content you promise in your podcast description and be sure to ask your listeners to give feedback, especially when starting a new podcast."—Linda Goldfarb

"Authenticity and providing value should be at the forefront of your approach. Stay true to your vision and voice, drawing from your genuine passion and expertise… Additionally, investing in high production quality, including clear audio, thoughtful editing, and a professional presentation, can significantly enhance the overall listening experience and leave a lasting impression on your audience."—Misty Phillip

"Look for trends in news headlines, statistics, and Google top searches. that align with your message and theme."—Tina Yeager

"Quality is in the eye of the listener. You know listeners find your podcast valuable when you find them recommending it to others."—Thomas Umstattd Jr.

"To provide quality content, it's important first to explore what type of content your audience is searching for. There are several ways to determine what type of content will keep your audience engaged:

- Poll your audience on social media to uncover felt needs.

- Do an internet search on what questions people in your niche are asking.
- Ask your subscribers what kind of content is of interest to them. What do they want to hear more about?
- Leverage your statistics to gage which episodes are most appealing to your audience—then offer similar content.
- Always vet your guests and validate your content. We build trust by providing true and accurate content."—Doris Swift

"I research! New books coming out, organizations that service my audience, newspapers online and in print, I look for fresh ideas and always incorporate the word of God. I also answer questions that are sent to me. I connect with like-minded ministries and share their information. Researching is the key!"—Lee Ann Mancini

"Ask your listeners what they need most. I love to have quick coffee chats on Zoom with my audience to see what they most need, what they are struggling with, and get their suggestions for future episodes. I review my stats to see if and when listeners are dropping off before the episode ends, which topics get the most downloads, etc. I adjust for the future to make sure it's not too long, and that I deliver on the promise of my episode title quickly."—Kim Stewart

"I stalk my guest! I listen to interviews they've done and search for a question that others haven't yet explored. When a guest says, "No one's ever asked me that before," I know I've done my job well.

I write at least ten questions for my 30-minute show in an order that makes sense to me. I pray and ask the Lord to show me a nugget of gold He's wanting to reveal through our chat. Submit your time to Jesus. His content is always quality!"—Sharon Tedford

"Do your due diligence in researching your topic of discussion and be well versed in it, especially if you're doing a solo podcast. The other thing I would add is to have a good mic with crisp, quality sound and good editing software."—Courtnaye Richard

"Your target audience is the best judge of your content. You want to ensure that what you produce is benefiting them and giving value. Asking for feedback and being open to constructive criticism are great quality control measures. Also, don't be slow to ask for help and support in the areas where you know you are weak. I am not good at audio editing, so I outsource that to someone who is good at it to improve the quality of the audio content."—Dr. Saundra Dalton-Smith

"Read the Bible. Seek the Holy Spirit's confirmation, and research what those who are seeking hope need to hear."—Jodi Howe

"Know your community. I ask myself, 'What do I want to learn about? What does my community want to learn about?' I want my clients to have resources, information, teaching, and inspiration available outside of our normal weekly session. As the podcast has grown beyond my clients, I found other ways to get to know my online community: (1) a private Facebook group (2) a subscription email newsletter (3) more dedication and attentiveness on Instagram. Within these connections, I ask questions and develop relationships, and every quarter or so, I send out a survey to check the pulse of my listeners."—Janell Rardon

Question 2

What can I do to help people return for more episodes?

"Give your listeners more than you promise. Utilizing your show note space, include downloads, websites, and content you can't cover in the episode. Include a next episode teaser during your broadcast and an invite to come back and bring a friend."—Goldfarb

"Engagement with your audience is paramount to building a loyal following. Tailor your content to address their interests and encourage interaction through various channels such as social media, email, and podcast platform comments. Involving your audience in your content, whether through Q&A sessions, listener stories, or polls on future topics, fosters a sense of community and connection. Consistency in releasing episodes is a fundamental practice for podcast growth and audience retention. By sticking to a reliable schedule, you keep your listeners engaged and eager for more."—Phillip

"Offer relevant and applicable content that helps audience members in areas they recognize as a need."—Yeager

"Make your episodes shorter. Listeners don't return for more if they didn't finish the last episode. Make your episodes valuable. Edit out all the boring and unhelpful bits. This might make the episode half as long, and that is good!"—Umstattd Jr.

"Your audience appreciates consistency and authenticity."

- Be your authentic self. People want to hear you and not someone you're trying to be.
- Be consistent in both episode length and episode release intervals.
- Be welcoming and intentional about asking people back to the show/ask for feedback
- Be sure to drop hints about future episodes to pique interest.
- Be proactive in asking people to subscribe so they'll receive notifications about new episodes."—Swift

"I always give them meat and not much fluff. People are too busy today. I want to share important information that will change their lives. I always offer additional information and links that are helpful to the topic being discussed."—Mancini

"I like to drop little nuggets of what's coming up in future episodes to encourage my listeners to return. My audience loves when I do a series of short episodes giving them small, doable tips in each one and they look forward to each one and often listen more than once. I also link to past related episodes in my description so they can find them easily when they hear me reference them. Also keeping a consistent schedule helps so they know when to look for episodes to pop up in their podcast app."—Stewart

"Make sure every episode fits my niche. Thereby, my regular listeners know they can trust the content they're about to get in each edition of the podcast. From time to time, I remind them to share our show with a friend though I don't say that every time because I don't want to be a nag. Our social media presence is largely interesting quotes and graphics from each guest to help new listeners find us, and to give our current listeners easy ways to share on their social media."—Tedford

"Consistency is king. If people get excited about listening to your podcast, they'll keep coming back for more. So, keep the excitement going by releasing your episodes consistently."—Richard

"When you choose relevant topics and keep your content engaging, it will cause people to come back for more. You can also try doing a series of episodes around a specific topic that walks people through a process. Each show builds on the next which creates a need for returning for the next episode."—Dr. Dalton-Smith

"Consistency is key to achieve loyalty and return listeners. Great content doesn't hurt either. Give them action steps if you are a Hope Provider, teases for future episodes. If you know you have a great guest coming on, and stories and testimonies for interests. Build a community through emails and a strong website with interactive communication and monthly newsletters. Take advantage of the free marketing you get from social media as well. People love to feel validated, so create a social media site where they can all come together to chat and support your podcast."—Howe

"Know your audience and know your community. As you develop relationships, albeit online, with your listeners, you will begin to naturally and supernaturally be directed to remarkable guests and inviting topics. As a solo host, I am the voice my guests connect with. Relationships and connection are everything here. Spend time strengthening your skills and developing great content that speaks directly to your listeners. Giveaways and contests are fun, but I've personally never seen any great increase as a result."—Rardon

Question 3

How do I prevent personally burning out?

"Never neglect your first love. My number one relationship as a faith-based podcaster is with the Lord. Keeping Him in focus, keeps me in balance. I can easily get caught up in the trappings of the business of podcasting and I've discovered by meeting with Father God every morning to talk out my day, I overcome overwhelm and reap the peace that passes all understanding."—Goldfarb

"Prioritize your well-being to prevent burnout. Manage your workload, schedule regular breaks, and respect your personal time, as this balance between passion and practicality ensures you have the energy and enthusiasm needed to consistently create compelling content. If you do decide to take a break, communicate with your audience and bring them along on your journey, demonstrating transparency and building a stronger connection. Your well-being is not only essential for your own fulfillment but also for the long-term success of your podcast." —Phillip

"Batch tasks. Work ahead. Take breaks. Connect with other podcasters in a supportive community." —Yeager

"Podcasting takes time and finding that time requires sacrificing whatever else you were doing with that time. If you sacrificed rest in order to start podcasting, you will burn out. If you sacrificed your Netflix subscription, you will likely be able to persist."—Umstattd Jr.

"Podcasting can be rewarding, invigorating, exciting, and exhausting."
A few tips to avoid burnout:

- Pray for direction and be intentional about Sabbath rest.
- Engage with podcasting communities for encouragement, invaluable info, and collaboration.
- Take breaks. Let your audience know you're taking a summer break/Christmas break.
- Reach out to a fellow podcasters.
- Ask for help—consider hiring an editor or virtual assistant, even if only temporarily.
- Make room for what brings you joy and feeds your soul; a refreshed host sets a positive tone"—Swift.

"I schedule my interviews two days during the week. I try not to overload my plate and it helps me to give the attention I need as an author to perform well. I pray for God's guidance, and ask him daily to give me wisdom and strength. I look for new subjects to discuss so I don't feel I am sharing the same information. I take time off when needed to recharge my batteries and every morning I am in the word of God."—Mancini

"I love to batch my podcast work. One day I'll work on ideas, and another day write out episode outlines. I like to batch record too. I'll usually block out one or two weeks to schedule interviews on several days, and to record my solo episodes. Then I can batch edit and upload. Also being in community with other podcasters is priceless to helping you avoid burnout. They are so generous in sharing tips about saving time and taking breaks and how to do that without losing listeners."—Stewart

"I have a co-producer and we agree to take off August most years. We re-spin previous editions so people who are new to us can have some great content put right in their inbox. We decided that although we'd have plenty of material for a weekly podcast and because this is a passion project for us both, and we both have other work to do, releasing an edition twice a month is enough. That gives us both space to work for pay which is a necessity and not be chasing our tails all the time."—Tedford

"The way to prevent burnout or pod-fade is to consider batching your content or episodes. Plan to record four or six in a week if you can, get them edited, write out your show notes, and schedule them for release."—Richard

"Pace yourself. I like to have periods of time where I record a lot of episodes over the course of a few months followed by a few months off. This way my weekly podcast show has a vault of new content ready to broadcast at all times and I don't have to stress during the months when I focus my attention on other things. I find it very important to get a lot of creative rest. Time in nature and enjoying artistic expressions like theater and music restore my creative energy and help me stay inspired."—Dr. Dalton-Smith

"Preventing burnout is hard, but I always suggest to forcefully take a break. If you're not at your best, your listeners will take note of that. There is nothing wrong with allowing yourself a few weeks off here or there or possibly breaking up your show into seasons so you can allow yourself the downtime needed. It's your show and you have free range to do whatever you feel is best for your audience and yourself."—Howe

"I ask myself tough questions: (1) What is my motive? (2) Why do I have this podcast? (3) Am I enjoying the interviews and content? If I'm not, my audience certainly isn't. (4) Do I compare myself regularly in a harmful way? (5) Do I obsess about numbers? And most importantly, (5) Do I still believe that God is in this work? If I move in my own strength and ambition and striving, I burn out and I typically get physically ill. Above all else, guard your heart (Proverbs 4:23), remember your why (Jeremiah 29:11-13), and find joy in the process (Nehemiah 8:10)."—Rardon

Take a moment to check out the Resource section. Visit the websites and podcasts of the podcast mentors previously quoted and observe their podcasting style. You won't connect with every host, but you will learn techniques that you want to incorporate into your own style. And realize some that don't work for you.

Beginning a podcast is exciting and can be overwhelming. Consider utilizing what currently works for professionals in the podcasting industry. What you absorb will most definitely shorten your learning curve.

I hope you highlight the tips you resonate with. Posting tips on sticky notes in prominent view reminds us to be courageous, to not give up, and remember we are not alone. If there was a podcaster's yell, I'd be shouting it right now.

You can do what you set your mind to. And if you need more help, consider a coach.

22

BEST HOSTING PRACTICE 11
Enlist a Coach

Is hosting a podcast your next best step? As a ten-year radio talk show host and award-winning podcasting host, I can take you from concept to a live program geared to your passion and personality.

Working with a coach dramatically increases the likelihood of reaching your desired level of success. According to the American Society of Training and Development, you have a 25 percent chance of achieving an idea you adopt on your own. But when you have an accountability partner to implement your plan, which a coach does, you will experience a 95 percent success rate.

Most podcast coaching would be a four-to-five-month agreement where you meet virtually, one-on-one with me eight to ten times for sixty-minute recorded sessions at least two weeks apart with unlimited email.

Depending on your goal, podcast coaching can include:

- Assessment of your current level of podcasting strengths and weaknesses
- Assess your presentation/personality style for the best-fit format
- Assess podcasting equipment needs and selection for your best fit
- Assess and choose the best podcasting platform
- Create an internal framework, prep sheets, scripts, and such for podcast
- Create twenty to twenty-five episode topics ready to record
- Create podcast trailer
- Perform audio postproduction
- Create Guest Interview Intake sheets
- Load your show on the top podcast directories

I'm an email away at Linda@LindaGoldfarb.com. Let me know if you've purchased this book to receive *Creating Dynamic Podcasts & Audiobooks* discount. Search for 'podcast coaching' to discover more options.

Now that you have read this chapter on the importance of coaching, I have a marketing bonus for you. When you check off the boxes of best practices, you can publicize your podcast to the world through a podcast launch announcement.

Launch announcements are usually emailed to media. Here is the text we used in the *Your Best Writing Life* podcast launch announcement:

Writers get ready to take your craft to the next level…

***Your Best Writing Life* Podcast** ~ (include launch date)

Whether you're a beginning writer or a bestseller author, we can't wait any longer to share the news!

The trailer for *Your Best Writing Life Podcast* is available on your favorite listening platform now.

Your Best Writing Life was born out of the desire of two storytellers, DiAnn Mills and Edie Melson, directors of Blue Ridge Mountains Christian Writers Conference, to encourage writers to follow God, embrace excellence, and write boldly.

After a long hiatus from her radio career, God has opened a new door—allowing Linda Goldfarb to get back on the air and host the show.

We've posted our two-minute trailer. Please take a moment to visit your favorite sites and subscribe. We encourage you to share with fellow writers as soon as you can.

iHeart Radio https://www.iheart.com/podcast/269-your-best-writing-life-69198117

Spotify https://open.spotify.com/show/3iUGyk1fhhnPpeowUOKbsD...

Apple Podcast/iTunes https://podcasts.apple.com/.../your-best-writing.../id1525394881

Our first interview airs September 1, 2020. Subscribe now so you won't miss one episode. Please subscribe and write a review while you're there. If you're familiar with the Blue Ridge Mountains Writer's Conference, you know the quality of our leadership and faculty. Let other writers know with a positive review. https://www.blueridgeconference.com

As a coach, I'm always thinking of your next best step. I'm so glad you took the first two steps—buying this book and reading it. The next step is to implement what you've learned.

It's time to celebrate and share your great new adventure with the world of podcasting. When you have your text solidified, create a PDF to post on social media and send to friends and family.

FINAL THOUGHTS FOR PODCASTERS

Don't allow the fear of failure or the fear of success to stop you from taking the necessary steps to begin your podcasting adventure. Don't tell yourself you will try your best either, as you keep in mind the powerful words of Master Jedi Yoda, "No! Try not. Do. Or do not. There is no try."

Ponder this truth. As you think, you believe. As you believe, you behave. All behaviors are either blessings or curses. May you always be blessed by the decisions you make.

AUDIOBOOKS

AND THE

FAITH-BASED WRITER

"Day to day pours out speech, and night to night reveals knowledge. There is no speech, nor are there words, whose voice is not heard."

(Psalm 19:2-3)

(((23)))

What Are Audiobooks?

Before you consider investing time and finances in the undertaking of audiobooks, consider how your book fits in this growing industry and who will work best as the narrator.

Let's begin with a little history of audiobooks and where they are purchased.

WHAT ARE AUDIOBOOKS?

Audiobooks date back to the 1930s. They served as an educational medium found in schools and libraries. Before audiobooks, often called talking books, were available digitally they sold in physical form on analog cassette tapes and vinyl records. Today, with the invention of the internet, audiobooks are now available from many different sources such as Windows Media Audio (WMA) and Advanced Audio Coding (AAC). The most popular format at this printing is the MP3 digital audio file download.

Listening to audiobooks is possible on a tablet, computer, home audio system, in-car entertainment system, or smartphone.

You purchase and download audiobooks in the same way as digital video and music. Audiobooks are purchased through online bookstores or downloaded free from public domain sites. Another outlet for audiobook downloads online is most public library systems —all you need is a library card.

LINDA'S STORY

"Have you recorded the Bible?" My new friend, Beth, stood inches from my face, both hands poised for prayer and a hopeful look in her eyes. "I could listen to your voice every day."

This wasn't the first comment made about my voice, but it's certainly the most memorable. And, no, I've not yet recorded the Bible in its entirety to the date of this publication. Though I've recorded a multitude of Scriptures via my daily *Let's Journey Together–a Moment with Father* episodes on the *Staying Real About Faith & Family* podcast. Though I'm not opposed to the idea of narrating the word of YHWH if approached by a publisher.

Audiobook narration allows me the opportunity to act without leaving the comfort of my home-based recording studio. I've enjoyed traveling and performing on stages nationally and internationally for nearly three decades. As a professional actress and presentation coach, I have the privilege of bringing stories to life personally and equip others to do the same whether in front of intimate audiences of one hundred and fifty or less, to full stage performances located in ten thousand seating capacity theatre houses. Actively using a variety of character voices over the years has primed me to bring life to the books I'm honored to record as well.

Radio and podcast hosting lends its own expertise to the venue of audible literacy, and I'm proud to spill out all I've learned over the years onto these pages to encourage and educate you in the arena of audiobooks.

One of the first questions I get when teaching classes on audiobooks at writers conferences is, "Can I record my own audiobook?" The simple answer is yes. But the first best practice before choosing the narrator is to discover how your book genre fits best in the audiobook arena.

Most, if not all, genres can work as an audiobook. That said, to know whether or not your book works in an audio format, let's consider the lifestyles of your reader/listeners and the content of your book.

(((24)))

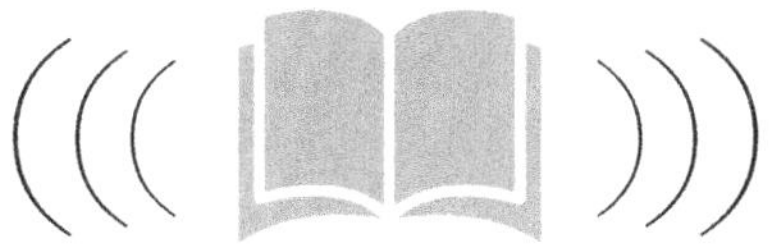

AUDIOBOOK BEST PRACTICE 1

CONSIDER YOUR AUDIENCE DEMOGRAPHICS

Audiobooks are listened to through technology. Therefore, your audience needs to have some knowledge of the digital world.

What devices do your readers use:

- Computer/laptop?
- Smart Mobile Devices – phones, tablets, or readers?
- Smart In-home Speakers – Siri, Alexa, Google Home, and such?

Are your readers listening while on the go?

- Commuting to and from work or school?
- Doing laundry? Cleaning house? Gardening?

Are your readers in need of audio assistance in their daily lives?

- Elderly?
- Impaired vision?
- Special needs?

Do your readers lead an active lifestyle?

- Walkers?
- Runners?
- Hikers?
- Treadmill or elliptical users?

Most audiobooks are accessed while commuting. This extended period, anywhere from one to two hours of listening time each way, is the perfect fit for audiobooks.

One of the latest polls shows, "Growth in American audiobook revenue by genre was led in 2021 by romance, self-help, and science-fiction, per the Audio Publishers Association."[6] (vi) The audiobook revenues in the United States reached $1.6 billion in 2021. Considering this fact, the odds are in your favor that your reader/listener will most likely listen to audiobooks.

CONSIDER YOUR BOOK

Audiobooks can average five to thirty hours of listening time, depending on the genre.

Questions you need to ask about your book:

Can your story hold your reader's interest for an extended length of time?

Would your book come to life under the prowess of a vocal professional or are you a good fit to self-narrate?

Have you listened to other books similar to yours in audio format? Are they popular with your listening audience?

Is your book better consumed at a table with a notepad and pencil as you read and ponder its content? If you are unsure, poll your readers and ask an industry professional.

As an audiobook narrator, I've noticed that many authors do not consider the audio option for their book until after the book has been published. With that in mind, I pose an important question: "Is your book written to be read audibly?"

If you have never read your book out loud, do it now. Or, have your computer read your manuscript to you. In this process, you will quickly discover the audio flaws that need adjusting prior to rendering your book into an audiobook. Don't fret when you find flaws, such as words that don't flow well one after the other. Finding audio issues now is the perfect time. Even if your book is already published.

You might think it's too late now, but it is not, especially if your book is published as an eBook. As digital downloads, eBooks can be updated. If you find the need to rewrite some of your content to flow better as an audiobook, you can do so with the electronic version and use this format for your audiobook narration purposes. Or, modify the PDF version of your final manuscript for audio narration only.

DOES YOUR BOOK HAVE AN APPEALING TITLE?

Audiobook buyers tend to be click-and-buy, not pick-up-and-look-first customers. Titles and book covers are immediate draws when it comes to audiobooks, especially if you are not one of the top best-selling authors who are known by name alone.

While you check out books in your genre, pay close attention to the cover design and titles. If your book is already published, this point is mute, but the title and cover should be considered with appeal in mind for books that follow.

(((25)))

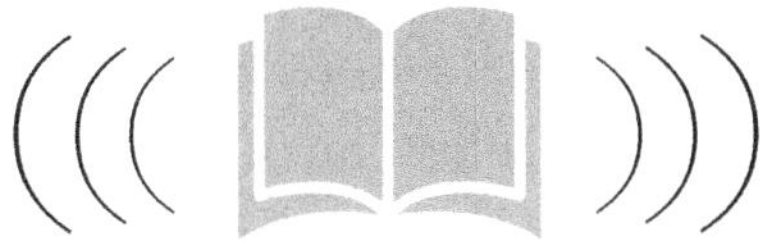

AUDIOBOOK BEST PRACTICE 2

BE DISCOVERABLE

Audiobooks are available at free and for a fee online retail locations. A best practice is to be available on as many as possible. Here are a few:

1. Apple Books: Audiobooks for iOS and macOS devices are available for download on the Apple Books app and store.
2. Audible: While audiobooks can be purchased individually, Audible offers a monthly subscription service that provides one free audiobook download per month. Use the Audible app for Android or iOS to listen on mobile devices.
3. All You Can Books: This site offers unlimited

access to thousands of downloadable audiobooks. This paid site offers the first month for free.

4. Rakuten kobo: This website offers the most popular and trending audiobooks for those looking for a good listen.
5. Nook Audiobooks: Barnes & Noble's audiobook website sells a large collection of audiobooks.
6. OverDrive: An app that offers thousands of audiobooks from more than 30,000 local libraries.

Links to each site are located on the resource page and more information is in The Matter of Money and Audiobooks chapter.

Every audiobook retailer charges a fee to sell your product, just like a brick and mortar store and other online outlets such as Amazon. The fees vary, and it is best to research the percentage for each outlet and how you will receive payment on audiobooks sold prior to placing your book with them.

(((26)))

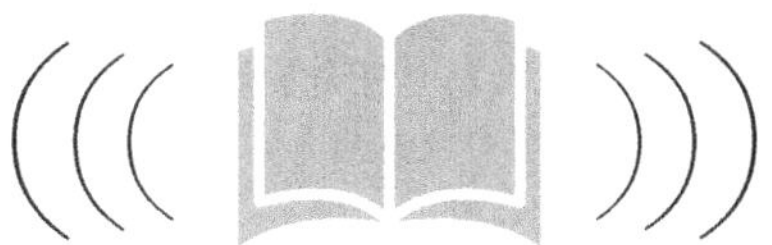

AUDIOBOOK BEST PRACTICE 3

Choose the Best Voice

Discover the best voice for your book.

Take a listen to audiobooks in your genre—you will not resonate with all of them, neither will your readers.

Self-narration or professional narration, that is the question. Several sources, like wiseink.com agree that some genres lend themselves to the author as a narrator. These would be memoirs, personal or family stories, and professional advice where the author is already accustomed to public speaking, seem to be good author narrated books.

Fiction, history, biographies, how-to guides, business, academic, or technical related books work well with professional voice actors. I've personally narrated memoirs and children's books for authors, so add these to the list as well.

A great resource if you are going the self-narration route is www.Blog.ACX.com.

SELF-NARRATION—DO YOU HAVE THE VOICE?

If your genre is memoirs, personal stories, or professional teaching and you've decided to go the author narration route, ask yourself if your voice is a good fit. To discover the appeal of your voice, record three or four sections of your book in an MP3 format. Most computers have recording software you can use for this purpose. These recordings don't have to be perfect. Consider these initial recordings as a rough draft of your paperback book. You know there can be improvements, but you're looking for the strengths and weaknesses in your presentation skills before you spend time and money in the full audiobook production.

Ask three to five beta readers who enjoy audiobooks to take a listen. Let them know you have several rough samples, and you want their honest feedback. Ask if they enjoyed the reading and what they liked the best. Ask what changes would help them enjoy the audio better. Did they like the pace and tone of the reading? Would they consider purchasing the audiobook with this narrator? If you prefer a blind testing where the listeners don't know it's your voice, have a third party enlist the individuals.

If the testers show promise to be listeners by giving you favorable feedback, then you have moved past the first hurdle to narrating your book.

DO YOU HAVE AN ACTIVE FOLLOWING ON SOCIAL MEDIA?

Another reason to self-narrate is when you have a large social media following. Now I agree that large is a relative term. If you have hundreds of thousands of followers waiting to hear your voice as an audiobook who are willing to pay $10 to $20 for a copy, then you may benefit from self-narration.

DO YOU HAVE THE TECHNICAL SKILLS?

Uploading your own audiobook is possible. Search online for tutorials to peruse the options. I utilize Findaway Voices. Findaway is an excellent platform for independent authors to hire a narrator and to upload their own narration for distribution. Be aware, you must have at least an eBook published on Amazon for Audible, the top audiobook retail outlet, to consider your audiobook for retail distribution.

Find the information you need to begin listing your audiobook on a retail platform in the Audiobook Best Practice 5 section under Retailer Info.

DO YOU HAVE A RECORDING STUDIO?

Your home studio doesn't have to be glamorous, but it will require a quality microphone, headphones, and the means to record your voice digitally. I utilize an in-home studio to record my audiobooks. The studio is a rectangle frame four feet long, three feet wide, and eight feet high, constructed of three-inch PVC pipe. A ¾-inch piece of plywood is bolted to the top to stabilize the unit. Four sides are draped with heavy-duty moving and packing blankets purchased from Amazon. ATS acoustical panels are secured to the ceiling and four sides for soundproofing.

My husband, Sam, built a shelf into the frame to hold my laptop and microphone boom system while I record. For lighting, I strung dimmable LED lights across the ceiling. I also use a tripod for my iPad to view the manuscript while recording. Finally, I have a tall stool to sit comfortably.

Find a Quiet Place. Closets work great for recording studios.

Sound Treatment. Moving and packing blankets, acoustic wall panels, and hanging clothes, all serve as sound treatment.

If a home studio is out of the question, rent studio time to record at local recording studios or radio stations. Studio time prices vary.

DO YOU HAVE A RECORDING EQUIPMENT?

Unlike podcasting, where street noise and the occasional barking dog is acceptable practice, audiobook narration must be recognized as a higher level of recording. The tools you need are a quality microphone, a comfortable set of headphones, and recording software. Be aware that new technology is right around the corner and what I list may be out of date when you read this book. That said, the information provided gives you a good start in what to look for and where to find it.

USB microphones that plug into your computer or laptop are popular and readily available on Amazon. A few brand choices to search for are Shure, Rode, Samson, and Audio-Technica. Here are a few recording tips that work with every microphone.

- Position your lips six to eight inches from the mic. Speak at an angle, across the mic
- Use a Pop Filter. Options include Flat Disc, Sock Type, or Semi-Circle
- Consider a Shock Mount to suspend your mic with a rubber cradle to prevent external noise associated from the microphone being bumped

For quality headphones, you get what you pay for. Headphone styles and types are a personal preference. I like mine to be lightweight and to plug into my microphone. Look for the best within-your-budget noise cancelling headset and try it out. If you are only recording one book, check the reviews from audiobook narrators and make your choice. A few brand choices to search for are Sennheiser, Sony, and Audio-Technica.

RECORDING SOFTWARE (DAW – DIGITAL AUDIO WORKSPACE)

I record my audiobooks on my MacBook Pro utilizing Adobe Audition. I use a Seagate external drive to store the audio files for my clients as the MP3 and WAV files can consume a lot of space on my laptop. MP3 and WAV are formats most commonly used to record audio files. Tutorials are available to explain exactly how to record these types of files utilizing the following recording/editing software. Look at:

Garage Band–free on Apple computers and laptops

Audacity–free software download for PC or Mac users

Adobe Audition – premium software download for the serious podcaster or audiobook narrator

VOCAL CARE FOR AUDIOBOOK NARRATORS

Vocal cord surgery is not pleasant. After damage from overuse and misuse, surgery was required to remove a few nodules from my vocal cords. The nonnegotiable seven-day directive from my surgeon for 100 percent silence included no clearing my throat, no whispering, and absolutely no audible sounds of any kind. I do have a crazy bat story, the winged version, that masterfully tested my resolve to remain silent. My seven-year-old son, Sammie, spent the night with a friend while I had surgery. He picked up a dead bat in their yard, and the bat tested positive for rabies. Taking Sammie to receive his gamma globulin injections within days of my surgery broke my heart. I consoled his weeping in silence. Unable to make a sound, as directed by my surgeon, my arms and tears became my voice.

Recovery after vocal cord surgery takes a toll on relationships. Relationships with loved ones and author relationships with contracted narrations due. What's a narrator to do? Include daily vocal care protocols. The following Vocal Care Tips for Voice Professionals that I learned aren't difficult once you develop the habit.

VOCAL CARE TIPS FOR VOICE PROFESSIONALS

- Stay hydrated. Daily drink one half ounce of room temperature water per body weight
- Use a warm steam humidifier. Gently inhaling steam hydrates mucus membrane
- Rest your voice for a few hours after prolonged use. Literally
- Combine a mixture of raw honey, hot herbal tea, and lemon. Drink to relax vocal cords

- Never make a sound to clear your throat. Instead, swallow repeatedly until you feel relief
- Refrain from drinking dairy and caffeine prior to recording

PROFESSIONAL NARRATION—IS THIS YOUR BEST CHOICE?

As a voice professional, I choose my audiobook projects carefully and usually allow time to record three books annually. Capturing the perfect voices for every client is my specialty and it's such fun bringing characters to life. Touring as a professional actress, broadcasting on the radio, and hosting podcasts for more than 35 years combined, proves that my voice has surpassed the test of time to draw in an audience, hold their attention, and leave them wanting more.

TIPS TO HELP YOU IN YOUR SELECTION OF A PROFESSIONAL NARRATOR:

Hear what the narrator offers before signing on the dotted line.

Ask potential narrators to provide a sample reading. I usually offer ten minutes to my clients, reading from multiple passages in the book. This allows the author to hear my versatility and my ability to capture the feel they are looking for.

Be sure your contract provides a specific start date, completion date, and check-in dates in between to make sure everything is on track.

Provide your narrator with an online location to upload your audios for easy access and review. I utilize Google Drive. My client has access via their email to review the MP3 audios. If changes, called pickups, are needed, my client writes them out in an email for multiple chapters at a time. The number of allowed pickups are determined between you and your narrator. On average ten pickups is a good number.

When your audio files have been successfully uploaded to your retailing platform, allow an additional thirty to sixty days for your audiobook to load on Amazon through Audible. You have no control over when retailers load your audiobook, and Audible takes the longest. Allowing extra time is helpful when planning your audiobook launch.

Market the audiobook just like your paperback. Enlist a launch team, street team, and beta listeners to get the word out.

BONUS TIPS FROM AUDIOBOOK NARRATOR PROFESSIONALS.

Question: What is your best tip to help authors work well with their narrator?

> "Choose your audition piece wisely. Provide examples of characters and scenes that you are particularly proud of, even if it is several excerpts from different parts of the book. The match made between your words and their voice needs to make

you feel good. Communication is key so don't be afraid to ask every question you can think of up front and know that you are entrusting your work to a professional. If there is any information you are holding back, about your characters or your passion, the narrator cannot use that in their artistic choices."—Ana Clements

"When hiring an audiobook narrator, you are hiring the voice of your brand. Do you want your book to be slow and thoughtful or full of energy and enthusiasm? Think of the 007 franchise and your favorite actor who embodied James Bond. Just like each actor brought James Bond to life differently, so each narrator will portray your work differently. Once you've chosen your narrator and have agreed on delivery of the sample they have provided of the audiobook, let go. Trust the artist you've hired to be the voice of your brand and bring it to life."—Sandra Murphy

"Be available for communication with your narrator, particularly if there are local words or idioms that the narrator might not be familiar with. Also, be willing to "hear" another interpretation of your work, besides the one in your head. Sometimes it will surprise you and will better serve to tell your story than what you imagine."—Michele Bailey

Question 2: What is the best tip for authors who want to narrate their own book?

> "Good acoustic treatment is more important than expensive equipment. Audiobook production is not as easy as reading into your phone. You need specialist recording equipment and an acoustically treated space to ensure you make a quality product.
>
> "Narration can be grueling, and it isn't a get rich quick scheme. Speak to people and find out what you don't know. Hire experts to do what you can't and create a quality product you can be proud of." —Clements
>
> "Work with an audiobook narration performance coach prior to recording for best vocal quality."—Murphy
>
> "Work with an editor or director. Having a second set of ears is so important."—Bailey

Your book's audio representation should capture your passion as the author and meet your reader's emotional and felt needs. Check the Resource section for information on the above narrators.

To locate additional audiobook narrators, search the websites of those you currently listen to and like. Findawayvoices.com has a list of narrators. Also, you can search 'audiobook narrators' in your specific genre.

I'm happy to talk with you about your project to see if my vocal wheelhouse has what your book requires to make a difference in the lives of your readers.

(((27)))

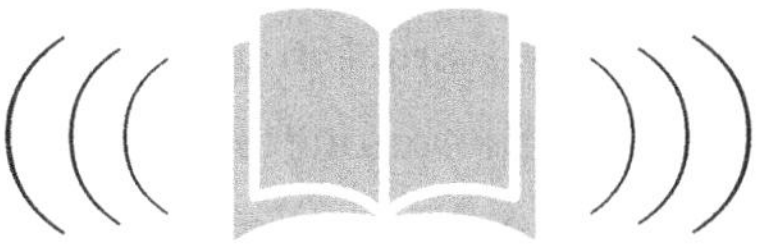

AUDIOBOOK BEST PRACTICE 4

The Matter of Money

Whether you record your own book or pay a narrator, there are fees associated with the production. On average a good to great narrator will cost between $150 to $300 per finished hour (pfh) of recording.

For every one hour of finished audio, the narrator will work two to three hours editing the audio to provide quality sound. For these prices you should receive ACX (Audiobook Creation Exchange) quality recordings ready to upload to your chosen distribution site. ACX is "a marketplace for professional narrators, authors, agents, publishers and rights holders to connect and create audiobooks."

Studio time is what you would pay as a self-narrated author. Find more on this in the Audiobook Best Practice, chapter 3.

Sound Engineer. Always enlist a sound engineer to master or finalize your audio files prior to uploading. Your cost will range from $50 to $150 and more per hour depending on the amount of work required.

Distribution and Uploading. You can create a free online account and upload your audios for free. You can hire out this process. Ask for referrals before handing out your hard-earned cash.

Cover Design or Marketing Pieces. As mentioned in the podcasting portion, Canva is a great resource to create your own artwork from book covers to promotional pieces. If you decide to do it yourself or hire this out, be sure you maintain your branding colors, fonts, and style for a cohesive look and to match your website.

HOW TO PRICE AN AUDIOBOOK

To determine your audiobook price, decide on the main goal. If your goal is to make as many sales as possible, then you want to set a normal retail price determined by genre and listening length. If your goal is to attract more readers and gain leads for your email marketing, set the price low to promote higher exposure. Be careful not to set the price too low and devalue your book. Better to start low for promotional or launching purposes and raise the price back to the average retail level at the end of a designated timeframe.

Consider the Audiobook Production Cost

Keep in mind how much you paid for the audiobook production and how many audiobooks you believe you can sell. For example, if your total production cost is $3,500 and you believe you can sell 350 copies, then set your price at $10 to break even. Professionally narrated audiobooks can warrant a higher price as the industry allows and based on the popularity of the narrator.

Consider Your Author Ranking

As writers we have an organic ranking wrapped around our popularity. Your best-selling presence in the book-buying market determines the ranking and influences the price of your audiobook. Best-selling authors with notable narrators can price their audiobooks at a premium. A novice writer is best suited to price their audiobook in the average range.

Consider the Length of Your Audiobook

Amazon offers pricing guidelines based on audiobook length. These are considered the suggested retail audiobook prices:

- Less than one hour: less than $7
- One to three hours: $7–$10
- Three to five hours: $10–$20
- Five to ten hours: $15–$25
- Ten to twenty hours: $20–$30
- Over twenty hours: $25–$35

The higher prices are geared toward the top tier best-selling authors. The lower price is good for authors starting out.

WHERE TO DISTRIBUTE YOUR AUDIOBOOK

Audiobook distribution is key to reach a wide audience, and it's not difficult to attain. I utilize Findaway Voices for my clients as Findaway offers integrated distribution on its platform. You do pay fees for any audio sold, but creating your account is free. Here is a sampling of distribution platforms. Use what fits you best.

Apple. "Browse, buy, and download audiobooks from your favorite authors on iTunes." https://books.apple.com/us/genre/audiobooks/id50000024

Audible. "Top seller of audiobooks on Amazon." https://www.audible.com/

Bibliotheca. "An intuitive and engaging digital experience that integrates with physical library activities." https://www.bibliotheca.com/solutions/ebooks-audiobooks/

Chirp. "Discover bestselling audiobooks for up to 95 percent off. Free audiobooks app with no subscription fees." https://www.chirpbooks.com/

Findaway Voices by Spotify. "Be everywhere, earn everywhere. This is the platform for independent authors who want to unlock the world's largest audiobook platforms." https://www.findaway-voices.com/

Rakuten kobo. "Our most popular and trending audiobooks for those looking for a good listen." https://www.kobo.com/us/en/audiobooks

Google Play. "This is the one app you need to buy and enjoy audiobooks. Choose from millions of the best sellers." https://play.google.com/store/books/category/audiobooks?hl=en_US&gl=US

(((28)))

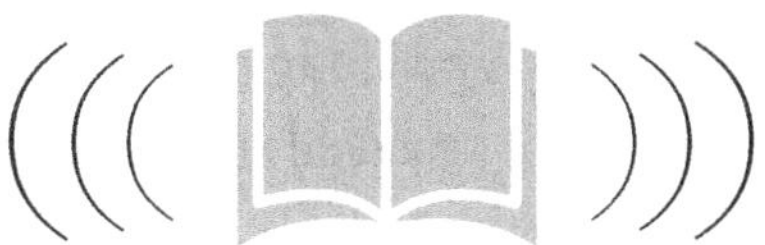

AUDIOBOOK BEST PRACTICE 5

Market Your Audiobook Effectively

Marketing your audiobook takes as much energy and tenacity as marketing the book itself. The good news though, is that you've already been down this road, and you know your product and audience well.

Consider bringing on a virtual assistant or a local person to help you navigate the marketing road. These individuals can manage areas outside your wheelhouse giving you time and energy to do what you do best, write.

Recording audiobooks for numerous authors has opened a door for me to educate others on this topic at writers and speakers conferences. Here are the top audiobook marketing tips I teach. Don't attempt to do them all. Find your best fit and plan your marketing around the launch and four weeks following the launch. Also plan for seasonal marketing to continue in perpetuity of your audiobook. Stay in front of your audience during the times best reflecting the content of your project.

BUNDLE YOUR BOOKS

Include your audiobook as an additional product to relaunch your paperback or eBook. Your Call to Action (CTA) can be: "Buy "name of your book" and listen to my audio version at a 50 percent discount."

COLLABORATE ONLINE

Recruit authors of similar genres to participate in an online blog tour. Bundle their audiobooks with yours as a Grand Prize.

Recruit authors of different genres to participate in an online blog tour. Bundle their audiobooks with yours as a Grand Prize.

Offer an Author Panel Zoom event "Five of the Friendliest or Funniest, Most Dramatic, Shortest, Tallest, Authors will share insider secrets about their books."

Create a Call to Action prompting the readers to interact with all the collaborators.

OFFER A LIVE INTERACTIVE EVENT

Invite readers to a local live event such as a book reading. Offer an audiobook at 50 percent off. Offer an online live event over Zoom, Stream Yard, YouTube, and Facebook. For your call to action or CTA, listen to the author's name, read from "book title," and receive a 50 percent off coupon for audiobook.

SOCIAL MEDIA VIDEO MEME FRENZY

Create meme videos with a sixty-second snippet from your audiobook. Post on Facebook, Instagram, Pinterest, and YouTube. Video memes can be created using Canva, they are also available through Buzzsprout.

SEASONAL/HOLIDAY/NATIONAL DAYS, SUCH AS CHRISTMAS, HOTDOG OR GRANDPARENTS DAY, THEMED PROMOTIONS

Select a day, week, or month related to your audiobook content and promote away. Create and post memes and pictures for designated themes with a caption from your audio. Always include a "what's in it for the reader" Call to Action.

AUDIOBOOK TRAILER WITH NARRATOR'S VOICE

Use snippets from your audio recordings in conjunction with video to form an audiobook trailer. Or provide your narrator with specific text to record promoting the audiobook.

DISCUSSION BOARDS, SUPPORT GROUPS, GOODREADS

Hang out where your audience hangs out. Listen, comment, share your thoughts. Don't sell. Become part of the family and when asked, let them know what you do. Being present in the lives of your listeners is the perfect gift.

(((29)))

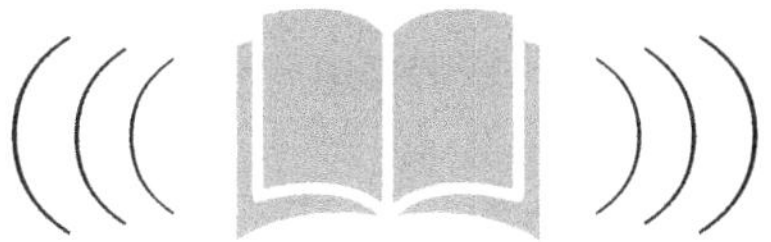

AUDIOBOOK BEST PRACTICE 6

Make Your Book Audio Ready

A book is ready to record when the author has taken precautions to supply the narrator with text that flows, storylines that flow, and words that flow clearly from their lips.

As the author, how you pronounce and mean what you write is critical to creating the best audio version of your book. Conveying your vision to the narrator is imperative.

One of my pet peeves as an audiobook narrator is when an author assumes everyone knows how they pronounce character names, locations, and those fantastic newly created fantasy creatures. Unless otherwise directed, most narrators will not take the time to look up correct pronunciations of well-known names, much less request the pronunciations of characters from the author.

So, supply your narrator with a pronunciation cheat sheet.

PHONETIC PRONUNCIATION SHEET

Create a phonetic pronunciation cheat sheet to assist your audiobook narrator.

Clear and concise phonetics are the surest way to help any narrator quickly work through your manuscript.

Here is an example from an audiobook I recorded for Robin Luftig.

For ease in reading on this smaller version, I have replaced the following categories in the chart with the associated letters:

A – Reference
B – Printed Word
C – Phonetically Spelled Word
D – Page in Manuscript the Word First Appears
E – Website Used if Needed.

A	B	C	D	E
1	Rupen	Rowo-Pen	8	None
2	Modi	Mow-dee	18	None
3	Wolter-storff	Wool-tear-storf	26	www.howtopronounce.com/dutch/wolterstorff
4	Harpham	HAR-pem	31	www.howtopronounce.com/harpham
5	Kopp	Cop	31	None
6	Nadab	NAY-dcb	32	None
7	Abihu	a-buy-who	32	None
8	Frankl	Frank-	49	None
9	There-sianstadt	Her-ese-see-in-statt	49	www.howtopronounce.com/search/german/Theresienstadt

To be sure you don't miss a word, create your phonetic reference sheet while you write, review, and edit your book, if you know while you write that you want your book in audiobook format. The page number needs only reflect the first time you introduced the word. Then, the narrator can seek the original word throughout the manuscript and replace it with phonetic spelling for easy recording.

SHORT CHARACTER SKETCHES

While you develop your characters in fiction or introduce non-fiction characters in your writing, write a short personality sketch for the primary and secondary players. This tool will assist the narrator in capturing the essence of your characters, ensuring they are portrayed to your expectations. Include the individual's name, age, gender, physique, personality, origination, culture, quirks, and meaningful attitudes.

A fiction example from Heather Kreke's book, *Path of Totality*.

Primary Characters

Jadzia(Jah-Dzee-ah)

- 17-year-old
- Female
- Dirty blonde hair, blue eyes
- Strong but thin build

- Socializer, talker/stabilizer, peacekeeper personality
- From north of Pittsburgh, PA
- Fluent in sarcasm

Brent

- 17-year-old
- Male
- Brown hair, brown eyes
- Strong build, works out
- Mobilizer, leader personality
- From north of Pittsburgh, PA
- Military man

Ryker (rye-ker)

- 18-year-old
- Male
- Blond hair, green eyes
- Average build
- Organizer, thinker personality
- From south of Nashville, Tennessee
- Outdoors guy

Secondary characters (Others I think deserve a unique voice)

Garrett (Gair-it)

- 24-year-old
- Male
- Blond hair, blue eyes

- Average build
- Mobilizer, leader/socializer, talker personality
- From Pittsburgh, PA
- Grew up wealthy

Sisko (sis-ko)

- 20-year-old
- Male
- Brown hair, brown eyes
- Average build
- Socializer, talker personality
- From Pittsburgh, PA
- Grew up wealthy

Cassie (Cas-sea)

- 18-year-old
- Female
- Platinum blonde hair, blue eyes
- Organizer, thinker personality
- From south of Nashville, TN
- Has a mean streak

Mr. Jenkins (Ryker's dad)

- 47-year-old
- Male
- Brown hair and eyes
- Stabilizer, peacekeeper/organizer, thinker personality
- From south of Nashville, TN

- Pastor, calm demeanor

Mrs. Mills (Jadzia's Mom)

- 48-year-old
- Female
- Blonde hair, blue eyes
- Organizer, thinker personality
- From north of Pittsburgh, PA
- Strong, calm

Character descriptions help the narrator visualize who you see and hear in your story. Bullet points are the perfect combination of brief and detailed descriptions.

AUDIO TONE AND STYLE

Narrators produce the best audio when they know the tone and style the author is seeking. In an audiobook, tone reveals the attitude conveyed through the point-of-view character by their specific word choice. For instance, you could show your characters attending a party and have the tone be sarcastic, excited, depressed, frightened, or hopeful. These emotions communicate the way the narrator should represent the situation verbally.

By presenting specific tones you desire in writing to your narrator beforehand, they can easily portray the feeling you want throughout the chapters.

You determine the verbal style of your book by sentence length, structure, position, and variation. The use of sensory details by including the five senses and figurative language, as in alliteration, rhythm, and repetition, gives the narrator a lot to work with to help bring the story to life. Style is not an add-on. While you pen your manuscript, include the above style concepts in the original writing.

UPLOADING YOUR AUDIOBOOK RETAIL INFO

Most audiobook retailers, such as Audible or Findaway Voices, need the following information to begin the audiobook uploading process.

Use a separate Word document to log the following items or check out the downloadable template from my website listed in the Resources section.

Book Title:

Book Subtitle:

Series (name of series and book number within the series):

Book Description (short, 400 characters):

Author Bio (You can use your back of the book bio, three to five sentences):

Author Name: as it appears on the book

Narrator Name: as it appears in the book

Publisher: as it appears in the book

Reader Age level:

Fiction or Non-fiction:

Language: English, Spanish, etc.

Primary BISAC Categories. Choose two and a corresponding subcategory at this link, https://bisg.org/page/BISACEdition Record your categories and subcategories from the list:

Awards earned for the book:

Key Words. Choose seven words a reader would enter in a Google search to find your book. For example, if you had a historical fiction book, you might choose 1830, historical, Georgia, plantation, slavery, romance, southern.

Source (Book) Copyright year and Owner: Either the author or publisher

Audio Copyright year and Owner: Either the author or publisher

Retail list price: Retail prices are usually suggested based on the genre and length of the audio.

Library List Price: This price is usually double the retail price as the library purchases it for multiple uses.

Launch Retail price: This would be the reduced price at launch if you offer a reduced rate.

Your Print Book ISBN: From your published book format.

Your eBook ISBN: From your eBook format.

Audiobook ISBN (Retail): Add this from ISBNs you purchase through Bowker or use assigned ISBNs offered by the distribution site.

Audiobook ISBN (Library): Add this from ISBNs you purchase through Bowker or use the assigned ISBN offered by the distribution site.

With this information, you can proceed to your chosen distribution platform and begin your author adventure into audiobooks.

FINAL THOUGHTS FOR AUDIOBOOK AUTHORS

Producing a quality audiobook takes an investment of time and finances. Time is a commodity you control, and a budget is something you can create.

TIME IS A COMMODITY YOU CONTROL, AND A BUDGET IS SOMETHING YOU CAN CREATE.

Enlisting the talent of a quality narrator is worth the down payment to book their time, even if it's to secure an audiobook launch in the future. Listen to several audiobook narrator samples to discover the tone, tempo, and feel you prefer for your book.

Copy the URLs of three to five books and note what you like about them. Reserve the data in a Future Audio Sources folder on your computer. When considering a narrator, ask if they can match what you like from the selected sources. Don't settle for second best. Father has the right fit for your book and the perfect timing. Pray for discernment and ask the tough questions without the fear of missing out.

ONLINE RESOURCES

Linda's Podcasting & Audiobook Templates for Download
https://www.LindaGoldfarb.com/the-writers-voice

Headliner Analyzer
https://aminstitute.com/headline/

Apple Books
https://www.apple.com/apple books/
Audible–https://www.audible.com/

All You Can Books–
https://www.allyoucanbooks.com/

Nook Audiobooks–https://www.barnesandnoble.com/b/audiobooks/_/N-2sgz

OverDrive–https://www.overdrive.com/apps/

Rakuten kobo–https://www.kobo.com/us/en/audiobooks

Audiobook Creation Exchange–https://www.acx.com/

CONTRIBUTING PODCAST EXPERTS

Thomas Umstattd Jr.
NovelMarketing.com
ChristianPublishingShow.com
Accepts guests

Doris Swift, Author, Speaker
Host of the award-winning *Fierce Calling Podcast*
Founder of Fierce Calling Ministries
https://dorisswift.com/
Accepts guests

Dr. Saundra Dalton Smith
I Choose My Best Life
https://I choosemybestlife.com
Accepts guests

Sharon Tedford
God in the Ordinary–(GITO)
https://61-things.com/gito/
Accepts guests

Kim Stewart, Book Marketing Strategist
Book Marketing Mania
https://kimstewartmarketing.com/podcast/
Accepts guests

Lee Ann Mancini, Author, Speaker
Raising Christian Kids
https://raisingchristiankids.com
Accepts guests

Tina Yeager, Author, Speaker
Flourish-Meant
https://tinayeager.libsyn.com
Accepts guests

Janell Rardon, Author, Speaker, Life Coach
Today's Heartlight with Janell
https://www.janellrardaon.com/podcast
Accepts guests

Courtnaye Richard, Speaker
Inside Out with Courtnaye
https://www.courtnayerichard.com/podcast
Accepts guests

Jodi Bilotti Howe, Speaker, Author
The Air That I Breathe
https://jodihowe.com
Solo podcast, no guests

Misty Phillip, Founder of Spark Media
Host of *By His Grace* and Co-Host of *Spark Influence*
www.SparkMedia.Ventures
Currently not accepting interviews

CONTRIBUTING AUDIOBOOK NARRATORS

Ana Clements, Narrator and Voiceover, Speaker and Coach www.anaclemnets.co.uk

Sandra Murphy, Audiobook Narrator, Voice Over Actor, Teaching Artist www.voicemama.com

Michele Bailey, Voice Actor www.michelebaileyvo. com

Endnotes

1 https://www.pewresearch.org/journalism/2023/04/18/podcasts-as-a-source-of-news-and-information

2 https://www.edisonresearch.com/infinite-dial-2023-from-edison-research-with-amazon-music-wondery-and-art19

3 https://www.pewresearch.org/journalism/fact-sheet/audio-and-podcasting

4 https://blubrry.com/podcast-insider/2019/01/14/3-surprising-podcast-stats-religious

5 https://www.buzzsprout.com

6 https://publishingperspectives.com/2022/06/audio-publishers-association-us-2021-audiobook-revenues-1-6-billion

ACKNOWLEDGEMENTS

First and foremost, I thank YHWH, Yeshua, and Ruach Ha-Kodesh (God the Father, Son, and Holy Spirit) for blessing me with open doors; no man can shut and closed doors; no man can open. May my writing be found worthy of Your call.

Thank you, Sam. Your daily prayers, hugs, and the together time you graciously relinquish to allow me to write, plus the many offerings of a bite to eat, coffee refill (frothed, of course), or a moment to stretch my legs as we walk to check the mail reassures me that I'm never alone and always seen. You are a blessing, the love of my life, and a fantastic husband.

Brenda Blanchard and Kelly Harris, thank you for always being there for me spiritually and relationally.

To my sister-friends, Edie Melson and DiAnn Mills, thank you for believing in me as the podcasting host for *Your Best Writing Life*. Your enthusiasm and encouragement refreshed my radio broadcasting heart to think I could do it, and years later, we have a two-time award-winning podcast with thousands of downloads and a faithful following. Praise the Lord!

The day Cheri Cowell asked me to step in as Audiobook Director for EABooks Publishing changed my future. I'm forever grateful for the chance to work with numerous authors over the years, narrate for some, and accrue narrators for others. Mostly, I'm honored to call you my precious friend.

Thank you to my Staying Real co-host and YBWL Associate Producer, Heather Greer. You make my job as a host so easy and such a joy. I'm blessed to have you in my life.

To my 4Sister Master-minders, Deb DeArmond, Debbie W. Wilson, and PeggySue Wells. Thank you for reviewing, suggesting, and editing this project. You are invaluable to me and my growth as a writer.

A shout out to all my podcast coaching clients, interviewees for *Your Best Writing Life* and *Staying Real About Faith & Family* podcasts, and the audiobook authors I've narrated for. Working with you has allowed me to make the mistakes needed to hone my craft and perfect my skills to present quality products for our audiences. You bless me.

To all writer and speaker conference directors who invite me to be part of their faculty to teach podcasting and audiobooks—thank you, thank you! I am honored to be included in the offering to provide faith-based creatives the opportunities they need to excel in their callings.

This project would not be in your hands without the encouragement and vision of my fabulous publishers, Karen and George Porter, my editor, Larry J. Leech II, and the Bold Vision Books family.

Finally, to those reading this book. Thank you for trusting me to come alongside you in perfecting your voice and increasing your territory beyond the pages of your writing. May YHWH bless you, keep you, and guide you in all you do to His glory.

Meet Linda

LINDA GOLDFARB is a multi-award-winning podcast host, multi-award-winning author, award-winning actress, and a much sought-after audio-book narrator. Linda's vocal prowess has impacted lives nationally and internationally from the stage, over the airwaves, and via the internet for more than three decades.

She emcees the highly attended Blue Ridge Mountains Christian Writers Conference and teaches on podcasting, audiobooks, and speaking at numerous writers and speaker's conferences around the country.

Connect with Linda at LindaGoldfarb.com

Made in the USA
Coppell, TX
21 July 2024

34975497R00118